MW01519682

Divorced

The Beginning of the End

MALLORY BROOKE

Tellwell Talent
www.tellwell.ca

ISBN
978-0-22887-976-3 (Hardcover)
978-0-22887-975-6 (Paperback)
978-0-22887-977-0 (eBook)

I dedicate this book to my parents.
Thank you for helping me get through this dark chapter in my life.
I will forever always be grateful.

TABLE OF CONTENTS

INTRODUCTION

$\int$his story that I'm about to tell you, reader, has been sitting in the back of my head and heart for seven long years. Seven years ago, a blonde-haired, bluey green-eyed, bubbly young woman named Mallory lived this experience. It is my story. A story that was supposed to have been about my dream wedding, to my dream man, on one of the largest luxury cruise ships in the whole world.

If you've followed my life online at all, you would know me exactly as I am, standing before you today, or rather sitting, I suppose, if we want to be truly honest here. Honesty is all I can give you and promise you, dear reader.

I honestly love adventuring in the forest and singing along to the classic sounds of mostly '80s and '90s music. I sing and dance my little heart out in the Canadian forest, in the middle of nowhere, on my Polaris all-terrain vehicle.

If you aren't already following me on Instagram, may I suggest that you give me @mallorybobalory a follow? I promise that you'll either laugh along at my fun, sarcastic entertainment or feel inspired and empowered. My hope for you is both!

My story of growth, love, heartbreak, and pain also has many comedic and ridiculous memories mixed in that will make me smile forever more. I was at a completely different stage of life; I was a lot younger (twenty-five years old, to be exact). I was naïve with the strongest people-pleasing tendencies instilled in my very bones and being, always trying to see the good in people and giving them the benefit of the doubt.

I find that there's more to the happily ever after story of what we all thought life was supposed to end up being in the end. Life's more about the journey, the ride, not just the ending of what society deemed the end goal: getting married to your one true love in the most spectacular way imaginable, having babies, and watching them grow. I'm divorced now. At this very moment, I'm dealing with divorce lawyers and splitting up assets from the past ten years of our lives. I'm trying to do this as fairly and equally as possible, navigating a new, cohesive, positive co-parenting role for our two little boys so that I don't disrupt their lives through my decision, my divorce…but I'm getting ahead of myself here.

I definitely had one hell of a messed-up journey. I've never opened myself up about the true story of what happened on the *Titanic*—that fateful seven days and six nights at sea, I mean. It's not as dramatic as it seems, as in nobody dies, and the ship doesn't sink in the end. Nevertheless, my heart sank, and I remember asking myself several freaking times if a camera crew was following my life around on that lovely ship.

To tell my story properly, I'll have to start at the beginning of this horror love story. This chapter in my story starts with a man named Atticus.

Part of the reason I am telling my story is to inspire my boys and people everywhere to break free of whatever is holding them back in life, whether that be society's expectations of which directions they should go in their lives or other people's expectations of them.

Just let them go.

Break free already.

CHAPTER 1

Atticus

How ironic that as I'm writing this novel, I'm also currently googling "Questions to ask your lawyer about divorce."

This love story turned dream wedding cruise ship disaster all started when a boy met a girl in a pub—an Irish pub in a small snowy Canadian city.

First, there was a spirited, fresh-out-of-college, hopeful, full-of-life blonde named Mallory. She was just out for drinks at a pub with three of her girlfriends named Annalise, Jessica, and Aurora. They were all sipping cocktails and sitting on cozy chairs by the pool table when suddenly, a couple of young, decently looking gentlemen popped up and took a seat next to them. The tall man with long blond hair had a guitar in his hand.

I, Mallory, was sick of them trying to impress us. Like, why did they bring their guitar randomly to the pub in the first place anyways?

"Can I try playing a little tune—a little somethin somethin?" I asked the tall blond.

"You don't even know how to play!" Aurora said, laughing.

Grabbing the guitar, I began strumming random notes and started singing the opening line to "My Heart Will Go On." Annalise, Jessica, and Aurora joined in because they all knew the song. "My Heart Will Go On" was originally sung by Celine Dion. I have a sick obsession with *Titanic* that started when I was thirteen years old in the '90s. Leonardo DiCaprio…that is all.

While I was strumming the guitar like the amateur rockstar that I am, a tall man with jet black hair swept to the side and beautiful brown eyes that twinkled when he smiled stopped playing pool with his friends and approached our couch jam session. He was dressed in a dark grey business suit with his tie hanging loose. He sat on the couch right beside Jessica and started chatting while trying to catch my eye. His laugh was infectious, and it made his eyes sparkle when he smiled. I immediately felt like a magnet was pulling us together. I wanted to get to know this mystery man who was making me feel some type of way—a way I hadn't felt before in my life up to this point, like fiery butterflies in my stomach!

Well, apparently, Jessica and this mystery man already knew each other from the small town where they both grew up.

"Mallory, meet Atticus. We went to school together," Jessica introduced.

"Hello there. I've heard lots about you!" Atticus exclaimed.

He had? Jessica gave me a wink. So it was her plan all along, I saw. Well, if anybody knew my type, it would be my best friend, right?

"You've only heard good things, I'm sure," I replied with a smile.

Soon enough, his friends all joined us at our table couches, and he finally got the nerve to come closer to chat with me. Atticus seemed highly liked by everyone around him. He was the typical life of the party, very easygoing with a witty sense of humour that I was immediately drawn to. His friends were also quite friendly and extremely nice. Not your typical douchebag type of men at all, which were usually the kind I was, unfortunately, attracted to—the bad boys. Atticus didn't give off any bad boy vibes. No, he was giving off something very different. This was what intrigued me the most, perhaps—his carefree, easy-going, friendly manly man attitude.

"Can I get you a drink?" he asked.

Sparks were already flying. He was the hottest thing on two legs, and I felt nervous being around him. I never got nervous; what was wrong with me?

"You may," I cheekily replied, and I followed him over to the bar. Immediately, we connected. He was intriguing, funny, and so sure of himself. We got to know each other. We had so many things in common: We both loved the outdoors, travelling, movies—weird sci-fi ones, to be exact. He ordered me a Ninja Turtle shot, which is gin mixed with some other concoction to make it turn green, like the '90s *Teenage Mutant Ninja Turtles*; it was delicious.

It was open mic night. On the tiny little stage, in front of the bar tables, Atticus's best friend started singing and playing his guitar. It was the song called "Wagon Wheel" by Darius Rucker! Atticus went up on stage and immediately joined in singing along with him. It was one of the most beautiful things I've ever seen. This man was so comfortable and confident, singing his heart out to this amazing song with his best friend on stage—so free and having fun.

After the performance, they both joined our table. Atticus sat next to me, inching closer and closer as we talked. The music was very loud, and it was hard to hear, but already, I couldn't get enough of this man.

"Congratulations on you're amazing performance, sir. I didn't see you as a country music lover," I joked.

"Country music isn't the greatest. My favourite band is called Against Me," he replied, eyes shining up at mine.

"I met the lead singer once. He told me I looked like a beautiful piece of man meat," he said, laughing.

"Oh my!" I laughed along.

"Where are we all going now!? Let's get out of here and go to the 9th Street house!" yelled Jessica, getting up from the table, holding hands with one of Atticus's friends, and clearly having a great night she didn't want to end. The 9th Street house was what my place was called because it was located on 9th Street, and it was the go-to after-party place.

Well, we all piled into vehicles and headed back to my house. When I say we all gathered back to my place, I mean like, seriously, all fifteen of us! Both his friends and mine, a bunch of easy-going, friendly Canadians at an after-party.

My house on 9th Street had a great big kitchen with bar stools around a sizable island in the middle of it. The large kitchen window overlooked the busy street that we were on. Although it had a nice big kitchen, every other room was tiny, so we were all cramped inside like sardines. This house wasn't in the best neighborhood, and it was on a very busy street, but the home was cozy, and the price was right!

Everybody, and I mean everybody, my friends and Jessica's friend, aka mystery dark, handsome man, all had a nice getting-to-know-each-other party at my first little house, basically an epic bachelorette pad.

Atticus was different. He was just so sure of himself and unlike anybody I had been with before, which was exactly what I thought I needed...what I thought I wanted. Atticus exuded confidence, and everybody seemed to clammer over themselves just to be around him, me included. He was so positive and free in the way he talked and walked. He was the epitome of Mr. Popular.

Atticus noticed a picture hanging on my refrigerator and pointed it out to me: a picture of my parents and me in front of Hogwarts Castle. This is a Harry Potter reference. Stay tuned; there'll be a lot of these in the upcoming chapters because it's another obsession of mine! I told him I had just gotten back from Orlando, Florida, visiting the new Harry Potter theme park, and I gave him a fair warning about my possibly out-of-control obsession. We were standing alone together in the dimly lit living room with painted turquoise walls, and the song "Gypsy" by Fleetwood Mac was playing in the background. I was pulling out my Harry Potter wand souvenir from its case to show Atticus.

"I love Harry Potter too! I'm obsessed. I've read all the books," Atticus exclaimed!

That was the moment I leaned in, grabbed his neck, and gave him a sweet kiss right then and there...and I was hooked! This kiss was magical, and I didn't want it to end. Atticus was an amazing kisser, soft and sensual, the kind of kiss that you long for days afterward. That was it for me. I already really liked this guy, and I just knew he was going to be my next great love...or so I thought.

As you can imagine, it was a perfect night.

I remember lying with Atticus one night, and the first time I almost told him I liked him was when we were falling asleep after making love. I said, "I'm falling in *like* with you."

"I know," he replied sleepily.

I lay awake, blinking in the dark silence afterward, unable to sleep, my heart sinking all the way down into my stomach.

Fuck, I should have known then...

We were inseparable, and we had that enthusiastic, fiery kind of love that comes out of nowhere, where you feel suddenly so attached to the wild soul, you would do anything for them and to be with them. Eleven months later, we went on a beautiful houseboat trip together in the mountains with my friends! I met his best friends that lived two provinces away. We travelled a lot, we adventured together, we were in a beautiful honeymoon stage of our relationship, and I had high hopes for our future. I was falling head over heels for this man the more time we spent together. He took me to a *Titanic* exhibition and indulged in all my nerdy interests!

After coming home from the mountains with Atticus, I headed straight back out west, travelling to the mountains again with my dad and his friends. I was very much a princess tomboy growing up, and I love the outdoors. This trip was our usual once-a-year fall ATV vacation before school. I felt pregnant on that trip. That's when I knew something wasn't right in my body. I took a pregnancy test as soon as I got back home from the quadding trip. Just as I suspected, yes, I was indeed pregnant.

I told Atticus first about my pregnancy. He was more excited than I had imagined. I expected him to be a little bit upset and disappointed like I was. Next, I told my parents, and I remember my dad asking me, "Do you want to marry this guy? Do you want to marry Atticus and be with him forever?"

Honestly, up until that point, I hadn't even thought of it.

I told him what every father wants to hear, "Of course I do. I'm excited to be with Atticus." We practically already lived together anyways. He was always staying overnight at my house most days of the week. He did work a lot of night shifts in a factory, so we didn't see each other often like normal people with normal lives and work schedules would. When he was sleeping, I was working, and then when I was sleeping, he was working— the dreaded night shift.

That was already a sickening part of the relationship, but I was now pregnant and having a baby with this man who I, so far, thought was kind and wonderful.

Fast forward to 2012, and our son, Callum, was born. The best day of my life, truly. Becoming a mother was all I ever dreamed of (besides also becoming a major pop star like Brittany Spears, of course). Now that Callum was here, it felt like it was time to plan our wedding. I didn't want to get married in a rush before he was born. I didn't want to be pregnant in a wedding dress. Maybe my heart already knew I shouldn't be marrying Atticus at all.

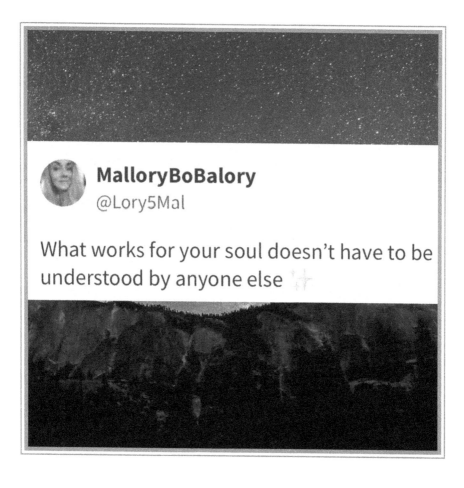

CHAPTER 2

The Proposal

Atticus and I were in Mexico with my wonderful parents, Viviana and Roy, on a family cruise ship vacation. Emma, my younger sister by one and a half years, also brought her boyfriend at the time, Patrick.

We sang lots of karaoke, had drinks, danced the nights away, and had so much fun exploring the islands; one was called St. Marteen. This tropical island is known for its soft sandy beaches, tourist trap excursions, and tons of shopping, especially for luxury and exquisite diamonds and jewellery. It has everything you would want as a Canadian tourist!

All of us were off doing our own things, excursions for the day. Atticus and I finally had a day to ourselves, so we immediately checked out the beach and then did a ton of shopping. Of course, I had to see what all the fuss was about! The smells of the salty ocean breeze and the sound of Caribbean music hung in the air. The aroma and vibe were intoxicating!

In the first jewellery store we went into were rows upon rows of sparkling beautiful diamond adornments. I was looking at all the diamond rings, and they were glittering around us, reflecting the shimmer off the mirrored windows along the walls. I walked toward a case that looked like it had one of Harry Potter's magical golden snitches in it. No, it wasn't a golden snitch or a philosopher's stone. It was a unique shimmery diamond ring, and it had me entranced with its rose-like design and a ton of sparkly diamonds. I was just staring at it and didn't really realize it until I heard a voice say…

"Do you want it?" Atticus asked.

That was the proposal right there…do I want it? Of course I wanted it. I mean, the ring was beautiful. Who wouldn't want it in the first place!? Second, I had already birthed Atticus's child, so there was also that. Third, we had been living together for years now. Atticus officially moved in with me once I became pregnant with our son, Callum. Callum was already one year old. Heck yes, I wanted that rose diamond ring and a commitment finally! I felt like I'd held this man's hand throughout his adult life up until this point already. He didn't know how to pay a bill, do laundry, cook, clean, or be motivated in any way whatsoever. I made the plans, I did all the things, so I never expected this man to look ahead into the future and purchase a ring. That wasn't in his nature.

So, he went to buy the ring, and I was so excited I had tears in my eyes. He didn't have enough money on him.

"Could you pay for it now, and I will obviously give you the money for it later?" he casually asked.

That wasn't the exact proposal I was hoping for, but I had sparkles in my eyes. The diamonds and my naivencss were blinding my ability to spot the red flag here. I had dreamed of this day my entire life since I was a little girl: how would my proposal be? Down on one knee? Romantic setting? Simple or elegant? A proclamation of love for me in some grandiose gesture like we read about or see in the movies?

We'd already had Callum together, so the next step naturally was to get married, right? We had lived together for three years, so I already had a clear idea of what kind of father and lover Atticus was.

If I had taken off my rose-coloured glasses before I walked down the aisle and asked myself the tough questions, then I would have already known in my heart that this man had a lot of growing up to do. He had a lot of soul-searching to do. I mean, don't we all?!

I was so excited; I didn't stop to think at all…like, what the fuck, Mallory? Nope, I was too damn excited! It was the most beautiful ring ever, and yes, I was engaged—finally engaged! (Side note: He never paid me back. I just found the receipt for the ring in my dresser the other day, in fact: $2,638.72 later.)

At the time, though, I was blinded by love and excitement, and I couldn't wait to tell my family! From the beach of St. Maarten, we hopped on the little fairy boat, which took us back to the cruise ship, and I was excitedly telling everyone about my newest engagement and the proposal. I showed off my ring on that boat, excited about life and my future with this man. I had felt we were already living the kind of married life that society expected anyways.

I told my family, who was beyond thrilled. We had a nice celebration dinner together in the a la carte restaurant on the ship. Then later, Emma, Pat, Atticus, and I carried on the celebration with cocktails and karaoke. Pat went onstage and sang an Elvis Presley song, and then I followed his act by singing Shania Twain's "Any Man of Mine." Then we headed to the disco nightclub on the ship and danced the night away! It was such a fun night and such a fabulous vacation altogether.

I was excited for my future with this man and our baby boy! Everything was coming together in my life, or so I thought.

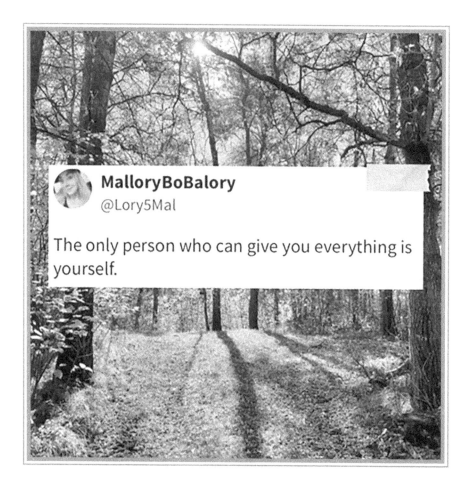

MalloryBoBalory
@Lory5Mal

The only person who can give you everything is yourself.

CHAPTER 3

Three Years of Engagement Later...

During those three years, I also took up a casual position in the hospital emergency to try to start the ball rolling for getting out of the tiny house on 9th Street and into a much safer neighborhood for Callum. So now I was full-time being an overachieving mother to my amazing son. I was also working four days a week and picking up shifts at Emergency in the hospital. I was exhausted but happy. My mother was taking care of Callum while I was away at work. We were so lucky to have her.

We didn't start planning for the wedding for three years. Mostly because I knew that I would be planning and doing, spending perhaps literally everything on my own as per usual, in its entirety. I was busy raising Callum pretty much on my own while working, while his father was employed out of the province for weeks at a time. I was extremely busy and also unsure about where I wanted the wedding to take place.

I felt like I didn't even have time to think about a possible wedding, let alone plan one by myself. Over the next three years, I was centered entirely around Callum (no change there, really). I was raising him to be the gentle, kind, wonderful soul that he is today! I watched Callum grow and become this spectacular little person! I was making sure that he had the best childhood possible, better than mine even, and I had the best childhood, or so I thought anyways! My goal in life was to be the best mother ever, and to this day, I hold true to that goal of mine.

Atticus, Callum, and I lived in the same rented little yellow house on 9th Street that I had previously been living in several years prior. It was a cute two-story house with a very shaded private backyard. Yes, indeed, the same house I practically had my first date with Atticus in—my "party house" we were still living in when Callum was born. We were trying to save up for a down payment on a place of our own soon, or should I say, I was the one saving up. I was the one making future goals and plans. Making any moves on all sorts of plans and anything, for that matter. Making anything move forward in any way imaginable. Just as I thought the way life should be for a small new family.

Atticus's work or occupation took him away for weeks at a time. So, it was usually just Callum and me. And so, I was also just waiting. I remember waiting for Atticus a lot during those three years that I felt he missed out on with our marriage and raising our son. He missed out on so much.

Callum and I were a team, and it was always my mission to make sure I also filled that void of his dad being away constantly.

I know I held myself to this higher expectation of motherhood because of it and over-exhausted myself to reach these unattainable goals. I had this idea that I had to be perfect for Callum.

Perfect mother, Mallory, filling his days, playing with him all the time, making sure he only had the best interactions and fun 24/7. I was overexerting myself so that maybe then, Callum wouldn't understand why his dad was not home, or why, when he was home, he didn't want to be around us. It was too much work for him to be a present father and attentive husband. He'd rather have gone out drinking with his friends that he always "needed to see" after all his time working away—not us, his little family. His friends were the priority. Not having responsibilities was his priority. His priority at the time wasn't me, his wife, or it wasn't his son, Callum. Nope, it was drinking with his friends and playing a shit-ton of video games.

During those three years, Atticus had a lot of growing up to do. Perhaps the most growing up he should have already done in his entire life before becoming a father and a husband. He moved too slowly through life, though.

We both had jobs; mine was in child welfare. I worked 8 a.m. to 4 p.m. four days a week so that I could be home more with Callum. If I had it my way, I'd be home with Callum all the time. Atticus is a geotechnical driller.

They take core samples from the earth to see if a company can build on the land, if it's safe to do so or not. For this, he has to travel all over Canada for weeks at a time. One specific time, I remember Atticus was away for three weeks in a row. Imagine three weeks physically away from your kid, your entire world, if your priorities were straight. Imagine how excited a three-year-old little boy would be. Callum was over-the-moon excited that his daddy was coming home, finally, after all that time, which would seem like an eternity to a young child.

It was 7:00 p.m. Friday night, and we were just settling down to watch the Disney movie *Aladdin* in the basement (we had matching PJs and all) when Atticus got home.

Atticus walked in the front door with his luggage, and we greeted him with enormous hugs and shrieks of pure joy and excitement! "Friday night family movie night!" Callum excitedly exclaimed, jumping up and down in his cute little *Aladdin* pajamas.

Callum and I had already picked out our movie and had popcorn made.

"Ohhh, I'll watch that movie with you guys tomorrow. I have to go to Ledger's tonight because Johnny's in town," Atticus replied.

I sat silently stunned and didn't say a word because I didn't really have much of a backbone then. I felt so sad and suddenly insecure. Why didn't he want to hang around us? Were we too boring for you, sir? This was starting to become a habit for Atticus: work away for days, weeks at a time, come home, then immediately leave to go out drinking with his friends. Time after time again. I bit my tongue each and every time.

"Actually, I have to hurry and get ready now. I'm already late," he said as he quickly raced around the house, trying to change his clothes and gather whatever alcohol he needed for the night. Typical. This scene playing out was, unfortunately, so typical of Atticus to do to us.

I could feel that lump in my throat just sink all the way down into my heart and then into my stomach. I had never felt so hurt and down on myself in my life. Why did this man not want to spend time with his son, who he hadn't seen in over three weeks? Even if it was just for an hour before his bedtime? What was so wrong with me that my fiancé didn't want to spend time with me either? Was it because I was not drinking? What was wrong with me?

Later that night, at three in the morning, Atticus came home drunk, woke me up from sleeping, and started arguing with me, his usual argument.

"Why aren't you happy I'm home? You should be jumping for joy," he said.

"Shhh, please keep your voice down. Callum is asleep. I was sleeping. Please just go to sleep," I pleaded.

It would be another hour before he would shut up and go to bed. At least he always had the common courtesy of not arguing in front of Callum; he always waited until he was asleep to yell at me.

I didn't argue with him. There was no point. This was still the time in my life when I was the biggest pushover, still easygoing but just scared. I was scared to argue with this man who almost never took responsibility, heard me ever, or even wanted to hear what I had to say. You know those types of people you just don't bother arguing with because you'll never get your point across anyways? That's Atticus. They always win.

He waltzed out the door, a bottle of gin in his hand, and said his "goodbye, see you tomorrow, we'll have a family day, yadda, yadda" words. Empty words and promises. I already had become too familiar with this man.

Callum and I were downstairs putting on the movie when Callum asked, "Mommy, why doesn't Daddy want to be with us?"

My heart, ugh, my heart at that moment. I hated that my three-year-old was having these self-doubt thoughts because of his selfish father. I swallowed that huge lump in my throat and told my sweet little boy how wonderful he was and how excited I was to have this fun movie night together. I was constantly making excuses for Atticus. It was exhausting. I did it because I knew that he was a great human being, just an extremely selfish one. A man who had a lot of growing up to do. A man who was already on that winding road of taking his fiancé and his son for granted, knowing we'd always be there. Thinking we'd always be there...

I'm not even going to get into the worst of it. That hadn't happened yet...but when Atticus came home, he always wanted and expected me to act a certain way. I had to be overly excited, happy, jumping for freaking joy even. I had to be on my best behavior when he got home from a stretch of a week or two of work. Otherwise, if I didn't, if I wasn't up to Atticus's "substitute my happy for your happiness" standards, then he would find something, anything, to yell at me about later, once Callum was asleep.

At least he respected one thing that I asked of him. That was not yelling or arguing in front of the kids, not letting Callum into that world of his dad's emotional, angry manic nonsense. At least he waited to abuse me mentally and emotionally until bedtime. That was the time I feared the most some nights, and I was already walking on eggshells.

I knew and appreciated and understood how hard he worked and how hard it must be for him to be away from his home and family for extended periods of time.

Happiness to me was spending time with Callum but also trying to afford a new house, in a nice neighborhood, with a good school for when that time came. My little boy had to go to a great school, which was important to me, living in a small city where I grew up my entire life.

MalloryBoBalory
@Lory5Mal

She was born to influence the world 🌍 not become like it

CHAPTER 4

Wedding Planning Begins

Three years of engagement later, I began the wedding planning process. Planning my wedding took about eight months of back-and-forth chats between the ship's wedding planner and me. Nicole was Royal Caribbean's wedding specialist.

The most appealing thing about a destination wedding was the simplicity of planning a wedding on a cruise ship, or moreover, having somebody *else* plan and do everything for me. I am not the kind of person who stresses over every single little detail or notices any details at all, for that matter. I could not care less about where the flowers would be and what we ate for supper, or what even the damn cake would look like. I bought an Amazon cake topper with Cinderella's princess carriage on top, along with Cinderella and her Prince Charming, of course! Easygoing Mallory just wanted everybody to have a smooth sailing, fantastic vacation, all getting along together.

You see, it was awkward between Atticus's family and my family. Not in a mean sort of way, just in the sense that we came from extremely different households growing up. I already cared too much about pleasing all my wedding guests when I should have been focusing more on the type of man I was walking down the aisle to. Yes, I loved this man truly, madly, deeply. This was what I thought love was—all-consuming co-dependency.

We were getting closer to the December wedding date now. Planning was ramping up, emails were going back and forth, and details were being ironed out. I was starting to show all my friends the pictures of my ship venue. The vows would take place on the top deck, inside the large, open-window, floor-to-ceiling city solarium overlooking the sea. The floor was supposed to light up down the aisle that I was to walk down, heading toward a wall of floor-to-ceiling glass windows with the sea stretching beyond. The music was going to be a soundtrack from *Titanic*, and it promised to be the most magical wedding ever—the day I had dreamed about since I was a little girl. The perfect wedding. I picked the "Royal Romance" package. So, everything down to the tuxedoes would be rented from the ship. Everything would be taken care of.

Congratulations! The Royal Romance team has received and approved your signed contract for a Royal Devotions package onboard Royal Meridian on the December 13, 2014, sailing!

WEDDING INVITATION:

You have been invited to attend Mallory and Atticus's Wedding on Royal Meridian!

Dec 13, 2014 – Saturday departure from Fort Lauderdale.

Eastern Caribbean Cruise

*Sailing Itinerary****

Day	Port ***	Arrive	Depart	Activity
Day 1	Fort Lauderdale, Florida	5:00 PM		
Day 2	Nassau, Bahamas	7:00 AM	2:00 PM	Docked
Day 3	Cruising			
Day 4	Charlotte Amalie, St. Thomas	10:00 AM	7:00 PM	Docked
Day 5	Philipsburg, St. Maarten	8:00 AM	5:00 PM	Docked
Day 6	Cruising			
Day 7	Cruising			
Day 8	Fort Lauderdale, Florida	6:15 AM		

*** All itineraries are subject to change without notice.

CHAPTER 5

Great Expectations

Although I knew of Atticus's faults, I still had enormous expectations for a happy married life. The perfect family life. The problem was that I was conditioned to just simply see past all of Atticus's red flags because we already had a child together. I already forgave myself for this: The not knowing any better. The thinking that my parents and society should tell me exactly how I should live my life and the order of events that it should directly fall in. The listening to people instead of my head and heart. The thinking that if I got married, then everything would fall into place with my relationship and life. This was the end goal of life for a female, was it not? To find a husband and take care of him for the rest of her life. I did not know any better, but I do now. I was younger then and a big people-pleaser. That I am no longer.

I also do not blame or fault my parents for their part in my upbringing into society's circle of life depiction that women are supposed to buy into. I empathize with my parents because they were brought up with those morals and values—mapped out in their minds to live out too.

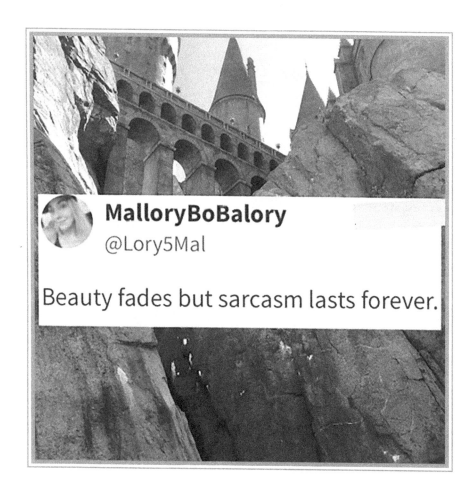

MalloryBoBalory
@Lory5Mal

Beauty fades but sarcasm lasts forever.

CHAPTER 6

Allllll Aboard

Day   1   <u>Fort Lauderdale, Florida</u>   5:00PM

*H*ello, sunny shiny Florida!

I remember stepping onto that ship like it was just yesterday. It was the grandest, biggest ship on the platform. One of the biggest cruise ships in the world at the time, the Royal Meridian.

I envisioned myself as Rose Dewitt Bukater from the *Titanic* movie, as she was dressed to impress, walking up the ramp into the most luxurious ship ever. That was me; I was Rose from *Titanic*, about to have my dream wedding on the most fabulous cruise ship in the entire world. What is life?! I was beyond excited. I was wearing the cutest short, white, flowy sundress, fit to perfection. My hair was in long beach waves, with my usual minimal makeup, natural look. I was about to embark on the adventure of a lifetime.

I had travelled with my future husband-to-be, Atticus, who oversaw all the luggage so that I could safely carry my beautiful Disney Princess wedding dress on the airplane with me, carry-on all the way. It was from the Jasmine Princess Collection, and it was a sparkly and shiny, beaded-to-perfection, form-fitting mermaid-style, with a slight princess flare, dazzling wedding dress. Let me tell you, it's quite the thing to transport your wedding dress through carry-on and airport security—concealing it, keeping it a secret from everybody while also handling all your other luggage and steering a toddler.

I couldn't wait to get into our room, put my dress away safe and sound, and relax after travelling with a two-year-old, my parents, Viviana and Roy Brooke, my sister Emma and my brother-in-law, Ledger. So, it was the seven of us. I had felt like a little fish in the great big ocean, standing on that Florida dock, surrounded by these marvelous gigantic ships. I'd never felt so small in my entire life. Well, besides that one time I escaped to New York City on a whim with my best friends…but that's a story for another time.

Here we all were, having lots of laughs and fun together, loading ourselves onto the Royal Meridian cruise ship, walking up the steep ramp into the luxurious foyer of this grand ship in the Caribbean seas, about to embark on our seven-day Caribbean cruise adventure. Hope and wonder filled the air into my lungs.

Right before you board or step onto the ship, the crew members always take the touristy preboard photo with the ship in the background. Afterward, you carry on to your stateroom, where your luggage is already waiting for you.

Atticus's parents, aka my future in-laws, and, holy Hannah Montana, where do we begin with these two human beings?

My in-laws. Karen and Daniel Fisher. Thing One and Thing Two, as I used to rudely refer to them whenever I talked about them to my friends. I no longer do that because I no longer let these two miserable humans "get to me."

Karen was your typical overbearing, socially awkward, no boundaries respected mother-in-law. Sounds fan-fuckingtastic doesn't it!? *Nope! Red flag, Mallory!*

Red flag number one should have been the time I went over to their house while I was dating her video game-obsessed son, who actually lived in another tiny broken-down house, literally ten steps away from his mother and father's trailer. *Whew…* Now that I got that off my chest, ahem.

One afternoon, while I was visiting Atticus at his place, which was an old two-bedroom, neglected, dirty old rickety home, I was doing the usual, sitting on the couch, watching Atticus play X-box while he smoked a large amount of pot. On this day, Atticus stepped over to his parents' place to grab something to eat. While he was over there, Karen barged in like she always did and exclaimed in her usual bellowing kind of blaringly obnoxious yet shaky voice, "*Here*, I washed these for you," as she handed over a pair of my underwear. They were folded and clean, yes, but what the actual fuck!? Where had she gotten them from? Was she snooping around? Why?

"Thanks," I mumbled, feeling my face hot with fury.

What kind of pathetic boundary was crossed right here that I didn't have the guts to establish or the will to stand up for myself at the time? I should have taken my undies and ran right then and there. If only I could scream, *Run, Mallory, run!*

Another time, just to paint you more of a picture of what I was dealing with here, I was working two jobs, trying to save up money to put a down payment on a home for our small family consisting of me, Atticus, and Callum (who was a one-year-old at the time). I was in a bind for a babysitter, and my best friend Jessica did me a huge favor by watching Callum last minute while Atticus and I were at work. While we were out of our house, Karen and Daniel decided to stop by and pay Callum a visit, of course without letting us know or asking us beforehand, as people usually do. Not only did they not leave once they found out my friend Jessica was there babysitting that afternoon, but they sat down on our couches and made themselves at home. Karen then preceded to chat away to Jessica about her most recent colonoscopy and everybody else's ailments in their small town. These people have zero, and I mean zero, boundaries. I felt so sorry for my friend that day. She was already doing me a huge favor by watching Callum, and then she had to deal with Thing One and Thing Two on top of it all! This was, unfortunately, just typical behavior.

So that's a tad about my *ex*-mother-in-law. Fuck, I could write an entire book series on that difficult, passive-aggressive lady. This is my story, though.

Daniel is a toned-down version of Karen, but they are practically the same stubborn person through and through. He's always right; she's always right; no use arguing otherwise.

Stubborn and cheap, instead of flying from Canada to the tip of the peninsula of the United States of America for their child's wedding, they decided to drive thousands of miles instead. Thousands of miles in their very old Chevy truck, stopping at cheap-ass motels along the way. It was an adventure fit enough for those two, I suppose.

This proved to be not the greatest decision ever, as their transmission broke down during their trek, and they had to dump thousands of dollars into their vehicle. Naturally, this put them both in the worst mood ever upon arrival at the biggest cruise ship in the world (at the time). We heard their broken transmission story about one hundred times during this vacation before the ship even left the dock.

That was their mood. That encompassed Daniel's mood. He was angry; he was already furious upon boarding that luxury boat. You could see it all over his frowny old face.

Atticus's older stepbrother (by fifteen years) and his wife were also on the boat, Bruce and Carol Fisher, or as I called them at the time, "the normalish Fishers." They were nice enough, and we all got along. It's easy for me to get along with everybody, though. I'm quite a pleasant person.

Atticus's brother Chad was one year younger than him. He was also along, chatting with us in the grand foyer with his engaged wife named Stephanie. Both nice enough people. The kind of people, though, that always thought they had something to prove to everyone, that they were better than everybody. Kind of noses stuck up in the air at everyone else. The kind of people who would be charming enough, one on one, but would literally talk bad about all their "friends" and practically everyone they knew. So, the kind of people you obviously can't trust or ever really get close to because you're sitting there listening and thinking: Gosh, I wonder what they say about me?

This was fine with me; I had enough trouble trusting people as it was. I was good at playing nice and pretending in their world.

While we were all meeting in the grand foyer, excitedly marveling at the ship's sheer size and magic, there was Daniel and Karen complaining. They were furious about how much money they already had to spend before getting on this boat, which they had complained enough about in the first place, negative people that they are. That set the whole tone for the first night on the Royal Meridian, unfortunately...

Atticus turned to me and explained that he would escort his grouchy parents to their stateroom and listen to more of their travel grievances while I unpacked and got settled with Callum.

You see, our staterooms were close together, but not close enough. Maneuvering around on a gigantic luxury cruise ship is difficult at first, to say the least. It's basically a city at sea. So many things to do and places to see, waterslides to slide down, but all the staterooms are crammed together and tiny. You need a map for the first few days to find your way around, down long, winding, narrow hallways leading to each.

My family and I were all located on the same side of the ship. On purpose, of course. We were next to each other, so our balconies were connected, and my son, Callum, could go back and forth as he pleased. Atticus's family, on the other hand, seemed to end up being on the opposite side of the ship. Funny how the travel agent seemed to book us all this way...planned out perfectly: Fishers on one side, the Brookes on the other.

We all had our own little ocean-side balconies. It's the most serene, beautiful view to wake up to and walk out to on your balcony—feeling so small, in the middle of the great big ocean.

The ship's horn started bellowing loudly for our evacuation drill. All passengers must partake and be counted before the ship is ever to leave the dock. This way, all passengers know exactly which lifeboat to get on, at which muster station, and that there would, in fact, be enough lifeboats for us all. Safety first.

Soon afterward, we were all on the top deck of the ship, waving goodbye to the people that were on land, sailing away toward the beautiful horizon to our first amazing destination, the Bahamas. We were on this magical new journey of mine—the ultimate dream destination wedding of a lifetime.

We all gathered for our first meal together, which would become a nightly reservation at 6:00 p.m. in the main dining hall, full of every delicious a la carte dish you could imagine, Michelin Chef style! Some people go on cruise ships for the dining alone. The food is amazing. It's a constant feast!

Everyone was enjoying themselves, and I was too excited about my upcoming wedding to notice a few people who were not so impressed. Atticus and his parents were quite grumpy and irritated, perhaps from their travels, I thought. Callum fell asleep at the dinner table, and then, as I was finished my meal, which consisted of a mouth-watering sirloin steak, dripping with scallops and hollandaise sauce, I announced that I was going to take him back to our stateroom and go to sleep as well. I wanted my beauty sleep, of course. I had a very big day coming up, the day every little girl dreams about her entire life.

"No, no, no, it's your first night on the ship. You go enjoy yourselves, and we'll take him. I can't stay awake any longer," my mother argued, smirking.

She'd had enough of the Fishers for one evening, and I couldn't blame her.

Everyone took off to a lovely little lounge downstairs. It was blue and ice-themed; a smoke ambiance filled the room to go along with the chill vibes.

Atticus and his family were ranting and raving about something. I was so tired I wanted to go to bed—tired of listening to all the negativity too.

"No, we can't go to bed so early on our first night," Atticus said. "Let's go for a hot tub, just the two of us."

Fine, a relaxing hot tub would be nice after this long journey. Then afterward, we could get right to bed so we could get up early to explore the Bahamas. The ship would be docked there for the entire next day for us to adventure around. I couldn't wait to hit up the cute little shops and check out the Caribbean island with Callum and, of course, the beach.

We said goodnight to everyone and headed back to our staterooms to change into our bathing suits. There were many hot tubs located on the ship, which were all situated on the top deck by the pool and waterslides. Little bars were near each pool and hot tub. It felt like there was a bar every ten steps you took on this cruise.

If only we had just stayed in our stateroom for the night. The late-night hot tub dip was the start of my troubles…

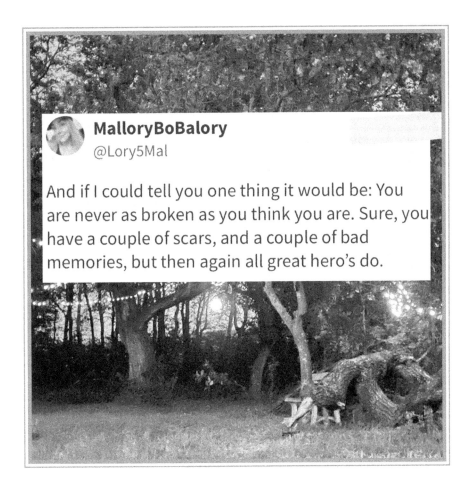

MalloryBoBalory
@Lory5Mal

And if I could tell you one thing it would be: You are never as broken as you think you are. Sure, you have a couple of scars, and a couple of bad memories, but then again all great hero's do.

CHAPTER 7

Ocean Hot Tub Under the Stars

If only we hadn't gone to the hot tub at the very top of the ship that night. It was beautiful, though, staring out underneath that diamond night sky, across a vast ocean. Simply Stunning.

It was just Atticus and me in that hot tub. There was a tiny bar right next to it and the pool area. Atticus was still having a lot of alcoholic beverages; he was quite drunk at this point, letting loose and having fun. I was glad to see him in a better mood because he was irritated and grumpy for most of the day.

About five or six tall, muscular men, likely the same age as us, perhaps a bit younger, entered the hot tub. They were drunk as skunks, immediately killing our relaxing vibe.

They all started chatting and were quite friendly. Atticus and the men were getting to know each other, and they told us they were Americans, from Boston to be exact. Atticus was chatting to these men about our wedding, the reason why we were on this amazing boat.

"Wow, I can't believe you guys are getting married on this cruise ship in a couple of days. That's so cool. What a great idea. Congratulations!" said one of the men with dark features and dark brown hair.

"Thank you! It's been smooth sailing so far. I will even get my tuxedo from the ship delivered to my room tomorrow. I don't have much to do; Royal Meridian literally takes care of everything," said Atticus.

I was feeling ready to go to bed and was wrinkled from being in the hot tub for such a long time. I told Atticus I was going back to the room. He said he'd follow me, so he started getting out of the hot tub with me.

The men wanted him to stay longer to party for some reason. They were giving Atticus a hard time for leaving. They wanted this party to carry on.

As I was drying myself off and finally escaping the hot tub's heat into the coolness of the late night, a couple of the men started heckling me.

"Canadian cunt" they yelled after me. Repeatedly, over, and over.

These men continued screaming at Atticus, name calling. It was strange, random, and annoying.

I rolled my eyes and continued toward the elevators. Atticus ran right behind me and was fuming mad that they were still calling me random names for no apparent reason.

"Atticus, they are obviously drunk and looking for a fight," I said.

I also told him, "Who cares what these strangers are saying? Everybody's way too drunk right now. Just walk away. I'm tired. Let's get to our room."

We continued walking toward the sliding glass doors off the top deck, which led to the elevators that would take us to the long winding hallway to our stateroom—home free. I just wanted to go to bed. Hopefully, everybody would be in a much better mood by tomorrow, and finally, the vacation-relaxation mode would be nice.

The doors were sliding behind us when we heard one last…

"Canadian c***."

"Okay, that's enough," said an extremely irritated Atticus, gritting his teeth.

Atticus stormed through those doors, and before I knew it, I saw him and one of the guys fist fighting. They knocked each other over and were now on the ground. I ran after him and couldn't get past the men surrounding the fight, just egging it all on. I remember screaming at the top of my lungs, "Stop! Get off of him! Stop it!"

Finally, Atticus broke himself away from them, and I ran after him into the elevators. He was shaking, angry, drunk, and out of breath. Atticus was bleeding a bit from his lip, and his shirt was torn at the collar. What in the fuck just happened? I knew this wouldn't be good. Sure, there was nobody else up on top deck to witness this fiasco, but there were cameras everywhere on this massive ship. There was no way there wasn't going to be repercussions for physical violence on this grand luxury cruise ship.

I was sick to my stomach. I was mad at Atticus, but I couldn't speak a word. I didn't want to anger him any more than he already was. He was ranting and raving about these random strange men all the way down that hallway to our stateroom.

"Those guys just couldn't keep their mouths shut. As if I'm going to let them talk to you like that, or me, all because we didn't stay and party longer!? I can't believe this night happened, this entire day even!" Atticus was yelling.

It felt like everybody on the ship was already asleep, besides us and those men from Boston. I kept trying to hush Atticus until we were in the room. Once we got inside, I felt we were safe from any more drama from that already unnecessarily dramatic first day, two days before the wedding of my dreams.

Atticus immediately fell fast asleep. I kept staring at the alarm clock. I had a sick feeling in my stomach that something bad was about to happen. Surely a staff member was monitoring the cameras that were located literally everywhere on this ship. Maybe it would be too dark for them to make out the people breaking out into a fight on camera? I couldn't sleep a wink that night, just staring at those red numbers on the alarm clock, waiting until I could get up and see my son, Callum. Then, truly everything would be alright again in the world. Wouldn't it?

CHAPTER 8

Day Two - The Bahamas

Day 2 Nassau, Bahamas   7:00AM -2:00PM   Royal Meridian Docked

The sun was peaking through the curtains and starting to light up the tiny room. Suddenly, the phone rang. I sat staring at it, listening to the piercing sound emanating from it, already knowing in my gut that it was not going to be good news. This phone call was not going to be good news for anybody to receive at 8:00 a.m. on a luxury cruise ship.

Finally, I picked it up. "Hello?"

"Good morning. We'll be requiring Atticus Fisher and Mallory Brooke's attention down on the main lobby deck. Now, please, ma'am."

"Okay. May I ask what this is about, and right this second, you'd like us to come down there?"

"All I can ask is for your attention on the main desk, ma'am. Right away, ma'am. Thank you."

He hung up.

My stomach sank. I knew we were about to be punished for Atticus's outburst last night, but I did not know how. My anxiety was through the roof. Clearly, they had made out on those cameras who was in that top deck hot tub brawl the night before.

I shook Atticus awake. He was sleeping soundly like a baby still in bed. Must be nice.

"Atticus, we need to get up and go to the main lobby right now; it's about last night! Oh, my goodness. I *knew* something bad was going to happen because of that fight!"

36

"Calm down. We don't know what's about to happen. It'll be fine," Atticus said, groggily wiping the sleep from his eyes, clearly not understanding the severity of the situation at all.

We quickly got dressed and headed down the long empty narrow hallways. Most people were still asleep, enjoying their first night on The Royal Meridian—how fucking magical that must be. Meanwhile, I was following my soon-to-be-husband down to the ship's main hub to get reprimanded for…his immature actions last night, I do not know! My brain was scrambling, trying to think of what would or could happen. Would they take away his drinking privileges? Or worse…mine!? Would they make us cancel our excursions? I was really looking forward to our scuba diving in St. Thomas with Atticus in a few days. We made our way to the front desk…

"Mallory Brooke and Atticus Fisher. We were requested to come meet down here," I spit out.

"Oh yes, right this way with me," The lady behind the desk replied.

I hated that they already knew we were coming.

She led us behind the desk to a room with a big TV and four small chairs against one wall. Atticus and I sat in the chairs, and a man in a suit walked in.

"So, do you know what this is about? You know that we cannot have people fighting on our boat, so you are going to have to disembark today. The other men involved are leaving today as well, and no charges are being laid. If you would like to press charges—"

I cut off the man in the suit. "What!? Get off the boat that I'm supposed to be getting married on tomorrow!?" I screamed and choked. I do not know how I got these words out, to be honest. I could barely breathe. It felt like somebody just punched me in the heart and stomach.

"No, ma'am, you don't have to get off. *He* does," The cruise ship director said.

"When?" Atticus quietly asked.

"Right now. Grab your things, sir, and we will escort you off the ship. We have zero tolerance for fighting misconduct on our cruise ships."

My dream wedding was flashing before my eyes. It was all slipping away in an instant. That very instant. I was hysterical, to say the least. I fell to the floor, and Atticus grabbed me and walked me out of the room. I could barely move. I was numb. He was holding me while I was hysterically crying, making my way back down the long hallways to our room, two security guards following far behind.

We ran into my parents in the hallway, and Atticus explained what had happened. Tears blurred my vision, and I was beyond a mess. Words cannot describe the pieces of my life that were falling apart at that very moment. It felt like the end of the world.

Atticus continued explaining to my parents what had just happened. He was calm but upset, trying to hold back tears. My dad, of course, stormed down to the lobby immediately.

He would take care of it. Dad would figure it out, I thought. He would get it sorted out like he always did. Even with that fleeting thought in my mind, I knew that this time was different.

My mom was with Callum in their room next to us, trying to keep it together for him, for all of us. I was on the bed, completely falling apart. Atticus was packing and trying to comfort me. I could not even speak. Just sobs. Was this real life? Was this actually happening to me? To us?

Atticus started acting sheepish, and he kept apologizing to me and saying that he would make it up to me.

"Is there any chance you'd leave the ship with me?" Atticus had the audacity to ask. "Take Callum and leave?" I said. "No, he can stay," Atticus replied.

"With whom?" He never thought anything through.

"I don't know. Your parents?" Atticus said.

Selfish.

Callum, our son, was looking forward to this vacation, this trip, and the theme parks afterward, too.

"So, I grab him and take him home now because Daddy fucked up on the cruise ship? Thousands of dollars already down the drain, thousands more to lose because of Atticus's actions," I said, irritated and sad.

"Decisions, decisions. How are we to get home from the Bahamas? Fly home now? Stay the night? Are there any flights today? So, I just leave our families, everyone we invited and made come out here to see us get married? I just vacate too? And oh, please watch our son while you're at it, while I go sit at home with you, staring at the walls and stewing when I don't even know if I want to be with you anymore because of this!" I'm fuming mad now.

Atticus sat in stunned silence. He had a glazed, serious look in his eyes, suddenly angry at me with my response but sad and guilty about the situation.

"Let us just walk off this boat hand in hand in solidarity with your immature, selfish fucking actions. Not a chance in hell, man!" I painfully explained to him.

My dad came back with a sad and serious look on his face. I knew the answer before he even said it. My sister, my brother-in-law, and Carol and Bruce were standing with us now, catching up with the latest shitshow that was currently unfolding. Everybody was simply stunned.

"Atticus, I watched the footage. They showed me the tape of you just going at it on the pool deck, fighting. Like, you cannot do that on big fancy boats like this, let alone anywhere. I asked and pleaded with them to just let you have the wedding, and then we can all get off. They said no," my dad said solemnly.

Atticus had his head in his hands.

"They could even charge you, but they will not. Unfortunately, we are technically in another country, so they had to call the Bahamas police on board to see if anybody is going to press charges," My dad said in disbelief.

Just when you thought it couldn't get any worse, a police officer stepped into the tiny stateroom and started questioning us again about the night's events. She told us that the other men were not pressing charges. Did he want to press charges? No. Now he had to get off the boat immediately, right this second. She was going to escort him off the ship now.

Carol and Bruce mentioned that Atticus's parents were off the boat in the Bahamas already and that they would look for them. That was their escape, their way out of helping sort any of this mess out. Emma and Ledger would take Callum to the pool to keep him distracted and away from all this nonsense.

My dad gave Atticus a big hug and told him he would come with him and figure out how to get him home. I could not watch Atticus walk off the boat because my heart was already breaking—broken. I gave Atticus a huge hug. I did feel bad for him at that time, getting escorted by police and the ship's security guards down that narrow hallway. I can picture this very clearly in my mind still to this day. I watched them all walking down that long hallway and then around the corner and out of sight.

I ran inside and threw myself over the balcony railings; it was dramatic. I was hysterical, screaming and crying for soooooo long. Crying out to the vast sea of emptiness where I thought nobody could hear me. My mom came over from her room next door and sat and hugged me while I sobbed for what felt like hours and hours. I felt numb and completely empty with thoughts racing through my head of what I should do about Atticus and our future together, what it would have been like to walk down the aisle in my wedding dress to this man, and what I was going to tell our son Callum. Was this the ultimate red flag?

I finally settled after what felt like forever, and then she lit her cigarette and passed it to me. I needed that right then, although I did not smoke cigarettes. We sat silently for a long time, dazed in disbelief.

"Should I have gotten off with him?" I asked her.

"Are you freaking kidding me? No, of course not. You did nothing wrong; he did this, Mallory. You did not ask for any of this. Besides, you two have your little son on board, who also never asked for any of this."

I already knew she was right.

My dad came back to the room and gave me a big hug. He had purchased Atticus's plane ticket home and helped him get a taxi to the airport. What a great man. He just took care of literally everything.

I started bawling again. "You've spent so much money and wasted more money on us. I'm so sorry. I feel so horribly bad."

He hugged me and told me never to worry about any of that. Now was the time to worry about myself. He said he was going to get a drink and find Callum by the pool. The ultimate best father and grandpa in the world. Callum was also the ultimate distraction because my family, at least, always kept their emotions under control around my little angel. There was no crying in front of him, and if a tear stung my eyes around Callum, if I could feel it coming on, I quickly threw on my sunglasses to cover up. I wanted to be strong for him on this trip and ensure he had the best time. The one solid thing in my life that I was one hundred percent confident in was that I was a great mother, the best mother that I've ever known. Of that, I am certain.

Mom and I were silently sitting stunned on the balcony, staring at the ocean, chain-smoking cigarettes, when the sliding glass door opened in my stateroom. In entered Karen Fisher, Atticus's mother. Great.

She explained how sorry she was that this happened and asked how Atticus got home.

I informed Karen that my dad had paid for a flight and taken care of Atticus. I was trying to elicit a thank you from her, thrown my father's way, perhaps some sort of payment back. Ha! Yeah, right! To this day, they have never thanked my parents for getting their son home safely and taking care of it all.

Karen continued going on about how I should try calling Atticus without delay. Also, did I want to get off the boat and look around the Bahamas? She carried on with her nonsense yammering when my mom finally shooshed her away, saying, "She doesn't need to do anything right now."

Shopping was the last thing on my mind.

I didn't want to talk on the phone with Atticus, as I was already wrestling with the idea of him leaving, but then, the thought of having Callum grow up without a father in our home was devastating to me.

By the afternoon, news of what had happened spread to our families. Callum came back to the room from swimming, and I bathed him and got him ready for the fancy a la carte dinner. We were playing with his trains on the floor, and I was so thankful that we were there together. Callum was obsessed with *Thomas the Tank Engine*. He had the entire fleet collection of trains from the TV show, which he loved so much.

Karen returned to my room, this time with Daniel. They gave me a hug again, and I thanked them. Then they proceeded to talk about the awful incident, and I had to stop them.

"I do not want this discussed around Callum, please. I mentioned to Callum that his daddy had to go back to work. He does not need any of this drama," I responded. Common sense, right?

"Are you guys coming for six o'clock supper still?" Karen asked hopefully.

Eating food was the last thing on my mind, let alone hanging around these folks any longer. I was not in the state of mind to sit around sulking in front of the families at dinner time. I did not want to ruin anyone's time or vacation any more than Atticus already had. I felt extremely guilty.

I told my parents to go, please go, enjoy dinner. I would be fine in my room.

They reluctantly left with Callum. Finally, I collapsed on my bed, sobbing. My head was racing with horrible thoughts about what my life would be like now, going forward, with or without Atticus in it.

Emma and Ledger returned to the room immediately after their family supper, and we had a long talk about their opinions on Atticus. It is funny to me that once people think that somebody may be out of your life for good, the real truths come pouring out. They revealed their secret thoughts on how they truly felt about our relationship, of how they felt about this man I was about to marry. Emma and Ledger made it so noticeably clear during the entire duration of the trip that this was a major red flag and to pursue an annulment. Problem solved, they thought.

"He's immature. He needs to grow up."

Absolutely true.

"He never treated you right. He was always making fun of you."

"He parties all the time and doesn't take responsibility for caring for Callum."

"He's an absent father and partner. You literally do everything."

"You and Callum are not his priority; he doesn't have his priorities straight."

"You can do so much better. He never deserved you in the first place. You're the best thing that happened to that Fisher family."

I appreciated how they told me like it was. Deep down, I knew their comments were all true. They also informed me that Carol and Bruce were talking and laughing about the entire incident at dinnertime. What the actual fuck? I was glad they found this all entertaining, at least.

Callum came back to the room, my little angel. Seeing his face then reminded me of Atticus. They have the same dark, beautiful eyes. How selfish would it be of me not to stay with my beautiful boy's father? I already felt mom-guilt to my bones. My parents, sister, and brother-in-law were all in the room with Callum and me. Trying not to cry, I told them that Callum and I would be fine tonight. It was late, and we needed to get some sleep for a fun pool day tomorrow. I was trying to lighten the mood for everyone.

I held Callum in bed with me while we watched the movie *Despicable Me* on TV. I did not sleep a wink that night.

CHAPTER 9

This Was Supposed to be the Wedding Day

*K*nock, knock, knock.

I checked the alarm clock; it was not like I hadn't been staring straight at it all night anyway, but the time was 7:00 a.m.

Who the heck would be bothering me at this hour on a world-class cruise vacation turned my real-life nightmare?

I sleepily got out of bed and headed toward the door. My heart was immediately in my throat at the sight of it: Hung on the side of my stateroom door was Atticus's groom's tuxedo.

Fuck.

Also, what in the actual fuck? Why was it there? How did they slip it in, and how did I not wake up to the sound of that happening? What was actually going on? Is this a dream, a really fucked up dream turned nightmare? Where are the cameras?

Ridiculous thoughts that mirrored my actual reality raced through my brain as I tried to internally calm myself down, quietly, as my son was still sound asleep. Let the sleeping little angel rest, I thought. Somebody needs to get some rest around here!

Atticus's tuxedo that he rented for our wedding, that was supposed to be taking place today at 11:00 a.m. in the promenade ballroom E deck, was hanging on the inside of my door. Just like the ghost that was supposed to be there right along with it. It was a dark reminder of what was not meant to be and what was supposed to be happening.

I was clinging to the tuxedo when my mom slid open the balcony door. Callum was still sleeping, so I whispered a "shh" and popped outside onto the balcony with her. Having Callum sleep and stay with me in my room forced me to be strong, to keep myself together, and get my emotions in check. It forced me to put on a smile and throw on some sunglasses— shades to cover up my puffy red eyes. I just looked at that sweet smiley face and remembered all was going to be right in the world as long as we had each other.

Fuck, if even staring out at the ocean with this view did not cheer me up, what would? Would I ever be genuinely happy again? All these pathetic thoughts went through my mind on repeat the entire time I was stuck on that god-forsaken ship—a gigantic living reminder of what wasn't happening.

"What else do we need to cancel today?" my mom asked as she shook her head in disbelief.

How did the ship not get notified somehow that this wedding was not going to be happening today? Thanks, Royal Meridian.

"Emma and I have makeup and hair in the salon at nine this morning," I said, sipping my coffee, trying to be normal that day. Whatever normal was. I just felt entirely numb.

"We took care of that," Mom replied, trying desperately to lessen my worry load.

Callum woke up and ran over to me for a big morning hug. He'll never truly know how much these big little hugs mean to me, I thought to myself, how much I need these.

I decided I was going to take him to the pool that morning after breakfast. I put on my huge sunglasses to hide my baggy red eyes, threw on a cute sundress over my bathing suit, got his stroller and pool toys ready, then set off down that hallway.

It took all my strength not to burst into tears around the ship or in the pool, especially when slow, romantic, or sad songs played over the speakers. I swear the ship was one gigantic slow song after slow song on repeat. Constantly slow, classic '90s Backstreet Boys ballads playing, singing about endless and everlasting love. Meanwhile, my love was sitting back in Canada, perhaps contemplating his entire life and how he's treated me. That's what I was wishing for anyways, a changed man. I kept envisioning myself slow dancing with Atticus in my wedding dress to these love songs. My mind was going back and forth from wanting romance with Atticus to wanting to push him overboard. Along with the oldies like "Stand by Me" sung by Ben. E. King, Callum forced me to be strong. I would not get upset in front of him. This was my inner mantra for holding it together. I would not get upset in front of Callum.

We had a nice morning swimming, and then we headed to grab some ice cream afterward. There were a ton of ice cream parlors located around the boat. After we had our ice cream, we ran into my parents, along with Emma and Ledger, who were currently participating in a competition of table tennis. We stopped to play and watch.

I was hyper-aware of the time. I could not stop looking at the clocks. It was 10:50 a.m. My mother noticed. I was shaking. I could not stop thinking about what was supposed to be taking place right then, which was me walking down the aisle to my favourite *Titanic* song, with the floor lighting up as I approached my future husband in the solarium overlooking the spectacular view of the ocean. Our family life would have been complete. It was supposed to be complete. A year's worth of planning down the drain in a single moment.

I was physically shaking at this point, and then up walked Karen and Daniel. She was hysterically crying and awkwardly gave me a hug, spastically pointing out the obvious, that we should have all been at the wedding at that very moment. My mom attempted to calm her down because she knew that I was trying desperately to keep it together.

"She knows, Karen. She is holding herself together here, trying to keep things normal for Callum. She has been staring at that clock," my mother calmly said.

Suddenly, Karen shoved her cell phone in my face saying, "Call him. You need to talk to him."

I backed off, gathering my space again, biting my lip. I would not cry. I would not cry.

"I cannot talk to him right now. I am so angry at him for putting my family and me in this situation. I do not want to talk to Atticus," I quietly replied.

She started arguing and dialing his phone number.

"Please stop this," my mother begged.

I slowly backed away and quietly asked my dad if he could watch Callum while I changed out of my wet bathing suit, back in my stateroom. I would be right back. He agreed that I needed to get away from that woman.

I sped to my stateroom, desperately holding back my tears. I was about to burst. Choking down the sobs was extremely hard to do with so many eyes and happy vacationers constantly around me.

Hiding behind my sunglasses, gasping for air, I told myself that I could make it to my stateroom for this inevitable breakdown, so I did not cause a scene. I was practically running to my room at this point. I closed the door and just let it all out. I grabbed the tuxedo hanging on the wall and used it to wipe away my tears. I could not stop crying.

I spotted something on the floor just underneath my door.

The wedding invitation.

The Royal Meridian crew members went to my family's rooms and my own and slipped a wedding invitation underneath each of our stateroom doors. Was this some kind of sick joke? Clearly, nobody notified them that the wedding was not going through today and that the groom was actually kicked off the cruise ship in another country. What a disaster. I was a mess, clutching the invitation on the floor, when my sister and brother-in-law walked in—they had come to check up on me. They picked me off the floor and took me over to the couch, where we all cried and sat together for a long time, just in a daze. Nothing seemed real. I felt like I was in a movie. Where were the hidden cameras? Ledger and Emma were trying to make me feel better by going on about how terrible Atticus was to me and how this was not supposed to happen.

"I could throw a rock down an empty hallway and hit a better man for you," said Emma—just a great one-liner.

I laughed; we all laughed. That funny quote, I will never forget.

Emma called the wedding planner and made sure she knew that the invites were a mistake and to please cancel all the rest of the wedding plans. Emma was informed that nothing could be reimbursed, so she planned for us to get our hair and makeup done another day. She came up with the idea that we would get drunk and have the wedding photographer take nice pictures of us around various parts of the ship together.

I was on board; I would do anything at this point for a laugh or a smile or to entertain anybody on this trip. I also felt entirely guilty about wasting money on all these events that would never take place now. Super people-pleaser Mallory. I felt so guilty for Atticus ruining everybody's vacation. I was angry at those random strangers who likely had no idea that the wedding was no longer taking place now because of that fight. I wished I would have said no to going to that hot tub in the first place. This professional photoshoot would be something extremely ridiculous but funny, sure to make everyone laugh, right? Even myself?

"Isn't that super weird to do, I mean, get in a wedding dress and have pictures taken even though I'm not getting married?"

"This whole situation is fucked up, and we will do whatever the fuck we want. That man has wasted enough of your money on this situation he created, so let's just do it!" Emma exclaimed.

Oh, the memories it would bring. Plus, it was Emma and Ledger's one-year wedding anniversary that same day. They could get nice pictures of themselves together and maybe even family ones. Then we would have cocktails simultaneously, and I would toss the bouquet of red roses over the ship! We were having fun making these silly plans. It was something to look forward to on what felt like to me, a cage at sea—jail ship. Do not get me wrong; I was so thankful to be on this amazing vacation and ship at sea in the first place. Grateful I was able to travel, but just perhaps not like this.

I changed into a black sundress with white daisies all over it, going for comfort and style always. We joined Callum and my parents to watch a newlyweds game show in the theatre. It was not funny to me, but I wanted not to be a sour burden to my family, so I pushed through the show and then left early with Callum to go swimming again. I did not want to watch happy couples ogling over their seemingly perfect marriages any longer.

Later that evening, Emma grabbed me for a wine-tasting event which was in the solarium part of the ship. Live trees and green foliage were in this certain area of the boat. It was nature at sea. It was beautiful and fancy. While we were tasting various types of wine, the staff was also educating everybody on diamonds. They explained the types of diamonds and jewels found on these islands and the quality to look for when we would dock at the ultimate jewel stop: the island of St. Maarten. I was soaking it all in, but I was not in the mood to drink. I knew that I was too sad, and if I were to get drunk at this point, I would just end up being a sad disaster. Good choices so far, Mallory.

Afterward, I was not in the mood to meet up with both families at dinner again either. I did not want to sit there and have them all gawk at me or shove cell phones in my face. I skipped out on the fine dining dinner with Callum, and we instead went to the "all you can eat" restaurant buffet together. It was not anything close to the fancy, stuffy, yet delicious six o'clock a la carte dinner everybody else would be attending. Nonetheless, I could not be around those people anymore that day. I just wanted alone time with my son. It felt like it took every ounce of my energy at this point to put on a smile and pretend to be happy so I didn't further ruin everybody's trip. I was exhausted, depressed, and my brain was racing, wondering what I was going to do with Atticus once I got off the *Titanic*, I mean, that ship.

My parents met with us after dinner and asked if I wanted to go watch the acrobats or one of the nightly shows. I responded with "no," and insisted they please do something fun themselves. Callum and I would have an early night, hanging out together around the boat and stateroom. We walked around, playing and exploring the boat.

Afterward, we snuggled up together in our stateroom and watched the movie that was on TV, *Madagascar*. He fell asleep on me, and I slept a little bit that night with Callum in my arms. This was all I would ever need, my little boy and me.

CHAPTER 10

Day 4 – St. Thomas Virgin Islands

Day 4   <u>Charlotte Amalie, St. Thomas</u>   10:00AM -7:00PM   Docked

This was the day I was supposed to go on a romantic honeymoon snorkeling adventure with my husband. I woke up bleary-eyed to the incredible mountainous view of St. Thomas. This tropical paradise should have filled my heart with excitement and joy. Instead, I felt a sincere longing. I was supposed to be going on a romantic excursion with my husband today…husband…that word. Wow, for the first time, I realized I already had a husband, and we were technically married. We had to sign the legal documents in our living room before our wedding vacation because you can't get legally married in the middle of the ocean. Our first big life event together had come to a screeching halt when he decided to use physical violence on a luxury cruise ship, letting his emotions get the best of him that entire day. That was something, I was realizing, that he tended to do quite often.

I got breakfast for Callum, and we sat and played with his Thomas the Train toys out on the balcony as I quietly sipped my coffee, staring out into the tropical abyss, trying to hold back another waterfall of tears for the day. I was thinking about how I would survive another day out there emotionally.

Emma and Ledger came inside, excited about the excursions they were going on that day. It was their one-year wedding anniversary: deep sea diving and day drinking, quite the magical combination. I was jealous but happy for them. They needed to have fun and get a break from the burden this ship held for us now.

"Look, we don't have to go. I feel bad going. We can stay…," Emma started, but I cut her off.

"Stay and sulk in my stateroom with me? Yeah, right. You two are going, and you will have the best time. It is your anniversary! Happy anniversary, by the way!" I tried to sound genuinely excited.

She smiled and gave me a huge hug.

"Do me a favor and enjoy yourselves today, please. I'll be fine with Callum," I said, and I meant it.

They set off to the island, and I told my parents that they better get off and explore St. Thomas too. There was no way, no how, I was getting off in St. Thomas. I didn't need to shop at the little stores near the boat dock. I had no intention of seeing and conversing in real life with real people that day. I wanted to avoid it all until…

Knock, knock.

In-laws.

Thing One and Thing Two were there. The Fishers were quite the hook in everybody's side. No pun intended.

"We're heading out on the island. Have you called Atticus yet?" Karen asked.

"No," I quickly responded, trying to immediately shut down the conversation.

"When we get back, we'd really like to spend some time with our grandchild. We haven't had any time with him, and you need to call Atticus," Karen said.

"When you guys get back from the island, you can watch Callum for a bit by the pool?" I responded, trying to compromise, and get them off my back for a bit.

Callum squeezed my hand at that moment. He was not comfortable with these people. He did not want to let me go. Callum has always had the most severe case of "making strange" with those people, his Fisher grandparents…hmm, I wonder why.

I wished everyone a wonderful day as I got Callum and me ready for the pool: stroller, blow up toys—check. Huge sunglasses to cover my huge red puffy, baggy eyes—check. I threw another cute sundress over my bathing suit, then pushed Callum's stroller to the pool, and we spent all afternoon playing together while most people were off the boat. It was quite nice having the entire pool to ourselves. We went to the ice cream parlor again and had a special treat and then watched the boats full of people coming back and forth from the ship to St. Thomas. We explored and adventured around the ship, pretending to look for pirates and buried treasure.

It was late afternoon when Callum and I rolled up to my parents, who were finally looking a bit more relaxed, drinks in hand, showing me their treasures from St. Thomas that they had purchased that day.

It was about time for me to drop Callum off with "Thing One and Thing Two" when they found us first on the very top deck bridge, overlooking the city at sea solarium, the middle part of the massive ship.

Karen was on a mission, cell phone in hand, already open. Flip phones.

"Have you talked to Atticus yet?" she asked. I had yet to even turn on my cellphone at this point.

My dad rolled his eyes, and I replied, "No, and frankly, I do not know if I want to just yet. I do not know what I am going to do about that man, honestly."

She opened her cell phone and shoved it in my face again. "Here!"

My dad stepped between us, in front of the broad, trying to stop her madness.

"Listen, she does not owe anybody anything. She did not ask for this. She needs to try to move on and have a decent time. This is her vacation, too, that he ruined. She is trying to continue calmly for Callum here," my dad said.

"I *need* her to call Atticus. She needs to call him," said Karen.

They started arguing full-on, and I quickly turned Callum around in the stroller and got him out of earshot of what was happening between his grandparents. My parents were arguing with my new husband's parents. Callum did not need to see his grandparents arguing with each other.

We were looking out at the ocean, and I was hoping, by some miracle, that maybe some dolphins would jump out of the water, and right at that exact moment, dolphins appeared. Callum and I were transfixed on the dolphins, who were playing games, jumping in and out of the ocean around the cruise ship—magical moments overshadowed by the distant arguing between my dad and my in-laws. Did I magically manifest these dolphins to appear as a distraction to my son at this very moment? I still believe so. Magical protection moment.

I saw Karen walking away crying as my dad and mom came over to us calmly and watched the ocean and dolphins with us over the side railings of the ship.

"Thanks, Dad," I quietly said. They each gave me a big hug.

"Well, the plan is to drop Callum off with them for an hour or two while we take you off the boat for a bit to shop around. What do you say?" he asked.

"Alrighty." I did not have any other choice, it seemed. I needed to keep the peace between everyone.

We stopped by their stateroom, I said a quick goodbye to Callum, and gave them a rundown of the supplies that were in the stroller.

"Have you been sleeping? I haven't slept at all; not one wink," said Karen.

Karen was being a spaz, trying to talk me into taking sleeping pills and bragging about the pills helping her sleep during this crazy time. She was going on and on about medication when I finally said, "I have my son sleeping in my room every night, so I don't feel comfortable taking sleeping pills right now with him in my care, alright?" I'd hoped she would act normal around Callum while I was gone for a short bit. This was already too much to ask.

I regretted leaving him with them, even if it was only for an hour or two. I hated that stupid plan of trying to get me off the boat for a while. Callum did not want me to go, but I assured him I would be back right away to get him. Today he is doing fine, though, and I tried not to linger on the goodbye before he realized that he was alone with those people.

Walking off the ship, I was struck by the loneliest feeling ever. I immediately wanted to cry as I pictured Atticus being escorted off the boat just a few days prior. I was walking with my parents off the boat and onto land for the first time in days. The clouds were covering the sun, and people were laughing and having an amazing time on the beach, splashing together. Suddenly I froze. I could not move. My feet were finally on solid ground, and I had suddenly felt like I was home, back in Canada, standing in front of Atticus, figuring my life out, trying to say goodbye. I kept having flashbacks in my mind—memories were flooding back. My mom asked if I wanted to go look in a certain shop. I reluctantly followed. My parents were already here all day, and I could tell they were desperately trying to take my mind off everything and putting up a fake happy "Let's have fun in St. Thomas" kind of front.

"I want to go back," I said. "I can't do this." I had flashbacks of the last time Atticus, and I were on this island together, much happier times.

I was also feeling guilty about leaving Callum alone with his other family, whom he wasn't the most comfortable around. Plus, why would I buy souvenirs to commemorate the worst vacation ever? I did not need to wander around. I needed to get off the boat and back to reality, back to my boy, my safe place. He was all I had now. A tropical island could not even cheer me up at this point. It was a cloudy fucking day on top of it all. Just like my mood.

By the time we reached Karen and Daniel's stateroom, Callum ran up to me excitedly with ice cream.

"Back already!?" they said.

"Yup, see you at dinner." I grabbed Callum, and we hurried back to our stateroom to shower and get ready for the evening: the first dinner I would have to force myself to show my face at, sit through, and get through. I decided it was time. Also, my parents had already discussed with me how I was missing one of the best parts of the cruise ship: the spectacular-tasting, fine-dining experiences and that I needed to eat actual food that night. They were worried I was not eating enough, and they were right.

CHAPTER 11

Meet Me at The Clock

F ine dining on a cruise ship. Emma and Ledger were not there that night, so I was stuck getting stared at by the entire table and family, the Fishers searching for some sort of reaction out of me. The pity stare—is there anything worse than the pity stare? Yet I still tried to conjure a smile. Nope, could not do it that night. I could not fake it. I was in a terrible, awful, sad, gloomy mood.

Mom and Dad planned with me to have Callum sleep in their room that night. That way, I could get out, walk around the ship, watch a show put on by the talented crew members…go where, and do what exactly? Do something, I suppose. Cry alone in my room sounded nice. Anywhere but here. I was ridiculously hungry, though. Now that I think about it, I can not remember the last thing I ate on this "all you can eat—all expenses paid" luxury cruise ship.

I finished eating my main course, a sirloin Oscar with pieces of seafood piled over top of the delicious medium-well-done steak and slathered in hollandaise sauce. I was tired of dodging stale questions and sour looks from the other side of the family all night. I was simply tired in general.

Suddenly, a note appeared on my lap, and I saw a giggly sister and brother-in-law sneaking away quickly, up and out of the restaurant. I opened the piece of paper with a pencil-scrawled sentence on it. A genuine smile spread across my face for the first time all trip.

Make it count.

Meet me at the clock.

This was a classic *Titanic* quote. Classic. My get out of jail free card. I showed my mother the piece of paper with our inside joke on it.

"In the movie *Titanic*, Jack Dawson goes to a ritzy dinner with Rose and her first-class crew of friends. Right before Jack leaves the dining table, he passes Rose this exact same note, and then they get into all sorts of shenanigans, really," I explained to my mother.

My parents were pleased that I was doing something on the ship, finally. I kissed Callum goodnight at the table and took off before dessert was even served.

Where exactly would they presume I would know to meet them? I suddenly remembered seeing a gigantic clock near the Broadway deck area, right in the centre of the ship. That must be the place where they meant to meet up with me.

They were there waiting for me right at the top of the stairs, near a gigantic clock taller than two people combined.

"Are you ready for a real party?" Emma smirked.

"Thanks, you guys. I appreciate you getting me out of there. You did not need to do this or involve me on your anniversary night!" I was so grateful.

"So, our plan is, we are going to have one drink at every single bar on this boat," Emma said.

"Okay, there are like over fifty bars, I'm sure, which is a lot, and I haven't really had a sip all trip so far. I am scared I am going to cry," I said.

"Cry. Go ahead and cry, just have some fun, let loose, and forget about all this, which none of it is your fault, to begin with. Let us make the most of this night."

"Okay, I agree," I replied, as Emma already had colourful shots lined up for all three of us.

I am not going to be hungover; I am parenting in the morning, I told myself as I swigged back a fruity cocktail.

We ventured to a few bars, had nice chats, and contemplated life and my relationship's future.

We headed to the piano bar next, always one of my favourites on a cruise ship.

I ordered myself a Long Island iced tea. A wonderfully talented young man was playing Elton John songs. We met five people our age who joined in on our infectious fun time and laughter, Hermoine, Mason, Michael, Jane, and Steven. All new friendly people from around the world. We were all practically sprawled across the top of the piano after a few beverages, singing along horribly, might I add, to the song "Crocodile Rock" by Elton John.

The next bar we went to was the casino. The sound of machines and the smell of cigar smoke filled the air, the atmosphere. Goddamnit, did I need a cigarette again. The cigarette my mother gave me before seemed to relax my nerves, and I was trying to numb one of the multiple feelings I was constantly experiencing on this ship! I really wanted one. We sat down and started playing slot machines. A tall, muscular-looking gentleman came over and started talking to me, but before I registered what he was saying, I asked him for a cigarette.

He took out his pack, gave me one of his cigarettes right away, and lit it for me.

"Thanks," I said as I walked away from him to go and sit with my friends, a cigarette and a cosmopolitan martini in hand. I felt pleased with myself for, number one, not crying, and number two, not having the worst time either. I was also just feeling drained.

Next up was the karaoke bar. The bar was jam packed full of people. I had a sudden urge to sing the song "You're So Vain" and, in my mind, recreate the scene where Andy Anderson from the early 2000s hit movie titled *How to Lose a Guy in Ten Days* sings about her breakup.

"It's full for the night. We have too many singers already," said a tall brunette young woman who was keeping track of the song requests at the karaoke sound booth.

"Woah, whoa, whoa!" Emma piped in. "If she wants to sing, she is going to sing. Mallory was supposed to get married on this boat a couple of days ago, but her husband was kicked off the ship for getting into a physical altercation."

There was always that stunned silence people had after being told the unbelievable tale. I get it. Disbelief and shock. I was obviously feeling all those emotions all the time too. It truly was an unbelievable story.

"Oh, my girl, you get on stage if that will make you happy," said the crew member.

All our new friends jumped for glee. They were all drunk, happy, and in a mood to dance and keep the good times rolling. So, being the fun people-pleaser I was back in the day, I would get up and sing a happy song. Even though I wanted to run out of that bar and go sulk in my stateroom, I took the shot that Stephanie had passed me and started for the stage.

I put in my song request. I was already next; I was already on stage. This was great because then it did not give me any time to really think and back out.

Emma, Ledger, and my friends were all in the front row and centre, yipping and hollering. They could not believe I had the guts to go onstage. It is not the attention I like; it is just singing and performing. And you know what? I'm actually a great singer.

I took the stage and grabbed the microphone. I was wearing my gorgeous, tight black mini dress. The perfect little black dress with a slight sheen, a sparkle to it. The lights went low, and a spotlight came over me on stage. Everyone was expecting me to sing a breakup song. That was not what came out…

"Black Velvet," baby.

I put on such an impressive performance. I felt like I was truly channeling my inner '80s Alannah Myles. The crowd was going wild! I honestly thought I forgot that I was meant to be celebrating with my future husband in the crowd right then, not those random fun, friendly strangers. Nonetheless, I followed up by singing Shania Twain's "Any Man of Mine." It took everything in me not to sing "My Heart Will Go On," by Celine Dion.

Let us end the night positive with zero tears in public today, I thought for my song choices. That was a goal and a win. Everybody was cheering me on and congratulating me afterward.

"You can sing. Like, you can actually sing, though!" my new friends excitedly exclaimed!

"Thank you, thank you." I bowed, brimming ear to ear.

A slow song started playing. The lights went low, and the next up onstage was an older lady singing her rendition of "You're Still the One" by Shania Twain.

Not a love song! I can't handle a love song right now… Time for me to disappear before I turn into tears! I thought.

"I am going to go." I gave Emma a big hug and thanked her and Ledger for the night. They walked me back to my stateroom, where I turned on the TV and cried.

CHAPTER 12

Day 5 – St. Maarten

Day 5 Philipsburg, St. Maarten   8:00AM   -5:00PM   Docked

*A*hhh, the beautiful tropical island of St. Maarten. St. Maarten was where Atticus and I got engaged two years prior to this nightmare. Remember my proposal story? So many people venture to this island for the beautiful white sandy beaches and the amazing jewellery, yes, the jewels. You can get a diamond for one-third of the price on this magical island because they were found here, mined here.

I was on a mission to buy myself something shiny, something sparkly, something more like retail therapy. I was eager to get off this god-forsaken boat that day. I was getting off the boat, even if it was just for a change of scenery, even though I knew the memories of the time Atticus and I were last there together would come flooding back. The time when we were celebrating our new engagement coming off the island, boarding the boat again. Now I was back there again contemplating the end before it had even really begun, well, the whole matriarch part of it, at least.

Thankfully, I did not have any excursions to cancel, just an entire day of shopping while Karen and Daniel got their chance to play with Callum on the ship. Meanwhile, my parents and I would go explore the island first, and then we would come to grab Callum after lunch. That way, the Fishers could take their turn shopping on St. Maarten.

We took a small ferry boat from the ship onto the main beach, where it was bustling with the sounds of Caribbean music, people laughing, dancing, drinking, and having a nice relaxing vacation. There were tons of brightly coloured, tiny, cramped shops lining the beaches, every one beckoning you, bribing you to look in their store.

Mom held up a shirt that read "St. Maarten," sized for a toddler.

"This would be so cute on Callum," she said, grinning.

"Yes, I really want all of the souvenirs on this trip, just so I can make sure I never forget it," I said, sarcastically smirking.

I was trying to smile and force a suitable time, so I was not ruining theirs anymore or wasting any more of my dad's hard-earned money. This vacation was something that we all needed. I took on the responsibility of feeling bad about Atticus ruining everybody's trip. Our families spent their time and money on this celebration we were supposed to be having. I felt so guilty 24/7 on this boat like I was ruining everybody's time. I was the one who had to put on a brave face whenever I would rather start bawling in the corner, with a Corona, preferably.

I was testing out my new knowledge about jewellery which I was educated in on the ship with Emma the previous night.

My mother wanted a new ring; she was obsessed with diamond rings. I was just perusing the jewellery aisles, Corona beer in hand, helping her decide right along with her.

We were at the second last store along the stretch of tiny shops along the beach when I spotted it, right there on the wall. It was gleaming so brightly by the sun shining directly on it as if the sun were a spotlight. I headed in the direction of this beautiful bright light. There, behind the glass on the wall, was a beautiful blue tanzanite necklace, almost identical to the heart of the ocean. That's another *Titanic* movie reference, readers. It truly was, though. Not near the same size as the acclaimed rare diamond that Rose was gifted on the *Titanic*, but similar enough that my parents both remarked how much it looked alike without me even speaking a word of it. I asked the man behind the counter if I could look at it. I glanced at the price tag right away and wanted to put it back. I could not spend this much money on myself. I could not let the necklace go, though, and I could not stop staring; it was like a magnetic force.

I set it down, thanked the shop owner, and then walked out of the store, chugging the rest of my beer, waiting for my parents to finish in that shop. I am a sucker for punishment, I thought. I should not want to hold this unattainable, too expensively gorgeous diamond any longer.

When my parents came out of the store, they were grinning from ear to ear. I thought, well, I am happy they're enjoying themselves; this is a good day.

My dad pulled out the necklace and put it on me.

"I love you; you deserve to wear this," he said.

I gave them the biggest hugs ever and thanked them to the moon and back. I had the necklace of my dreams. It felt like a million dollars around my neck and that it held some sort of magical powers. Magic powers to get me through this chapter in my life.

It was the sparkling light at the end of the longest dark tunnel.

CHAPTER 13

Day 6 – The Photoshoot

This day was a full day at sea. Emma and I had our appointment together at the salon on the ship that morning to get our hair and makeup professionally done. This was supposed to make up for the hair and makeup we did not receive prior to my "supposed-to-be" wedding day.

We sat in the chairs next to each other, getting our hair curled. I wanted my blonde locks halfway up so I could place my pretty sparkly beaded headpiece around the circumference of the crown of my head. It was almost like a flower child crown but with diamonds and beads. This was what I was going to wear with my wedding dress. No veil, I thought, just this gorgeous headband headpiece. I was a sucker for a good headband.

That morning, I had found Atticus's favourite T-shirt that he'd accidentally left behind, stuffed in the closet. I decided to wear it. It was black and had the band name, Against Me, written across it in sage green lettering. I did not enjoy this kind of punk music or this band at all. I decided I was wearing Atticus's favourite T-shirt to the salon. That day, I was mostly mad at him. Inside I was fuming angry flames at the man. I suppose that was my way of showing it. I wanted to prove to myself that I was one hundred percent over Atticus, and I would not tolerate his disrespect in my life any longer. That day I was angry.

Emma and I were regaling my tired and true wedding cruise ship disaster tale to the nice young ladies who were putting on our hair and makeup, which had already become the story of my life, I felt, unfortunately. They gasped and could not believe it. This is usually the reaction I still get to this day when telling my unbelievable wedding story.

I was drinking champagne, and getting my makeup done, yet I almost wanted to cry a few times when my sister was carrying on about how awful that man was. It felt like an out-of-body experience. Was this all happening right now to me? Angela, my makeup artist, could not get over the fact that I was wearing *her* favourite band of all time on a T-shirt. She absolutely loved it and talked so much about her love of their music. So, before Emma and I left the salon, we said farewell to the nice ladies, and I gifted Angela the T-shirt right off my back. (Do not worry, I was wearing a bikini top underneath my shirt.) I am always ready wearing a bikini on vacation underneath my clothes because you just never know when you want to or need to jump in a pool or ocean.

Angela had tears in her eyes; she was so thankful. This was her favourite band in the whole entire world. I knew Atticus would be furious at me for giving away his favourite T-shirt and that, in itself, was giving me all the satisfaction I needed to gift this T-shirt of mine, or his, I suppose. Emma was hysterically laughing; it might have been the champagne or just the hilarity and randomness of it all—a small, tiny way we could get back at him in a way. Yes, I was in the anger stage of it all that day.

We walked back to our staterooms to get dressed. I was wearing my wedding gown for the photoshoot, and Emma would be in her black bridesmaid dress. Ledger was in his tuxedo.

This was the first time I got to see myself in the full wedding getup: the makeup, perfect hair, the gorgeous headpiece, and the most beautiful dress I had ever laid eyes on. My eyes were tearing up, and I wanted to burst into tears, but I told myself not to cry, that I'd get to wear a beautiful dress like that again someday, and it would be more magical than I could ever imagine.

I was staring at myself in the mirror when my dad slid in through my balcony door. He first apologized but then started getting tears in his eyes and gave me a big hug.

"I'm so sorry," was all he could say. He was extremely choked up, catching the tears in his throat before they reached the air.

"Are you and Mom not coming to get pictures?" I asked.

"It's too hard for your mother and I to see you like this, and all we want to do is spend time at the pool having fun with Callum today," said my bleary-eyed father.

I understood completely, as I had done the same with Callum for most of the trip so far. They wanted us to have fun with this—a fun photoshoot day.

Emma, Ledger, and I met up with the photographer and started going to various parts of the ship to take photos. I absolutely loved walking around in my flowy dress, finding a reason to finally wear this beautiful Disney Princess wedding gown that was made just for me.

We took combination pictures. Emma and Ledger took nice photos together, and we had so many drinks and laughs. A lot of people on the ship stopped to let me know how beautiful they thought it all was. I'm sure they were also trying to figure out who was marrying whom, one of perhaps the funniest parts of it all, I thought.

Our new friendly friends—Stephanie, Mason, Michael, Jane, and Steven—that we met at the bar-hopping, karaoke night, ran into us during the photoshoot session and joined along on our random fun. The five of them were also dressed to impress as the nightly theme for dinner that night was casino night. Fancy dress night. We were all ready to go, dressed to impress, taking shots in our dresses, taking photographs, and having a wonderful time.

One final photo was me tossing the bouquet of red roses, right off the bow of the ship. I realize this is all very silly and super dramatic and yet at the time, oh so necessary. The roses symbolized my wedding, which I felt like I was quite literally throwing overboard, letting it go.

We were finally smiling and genuinely laughing. The photographer said goodbye and we all sat at the bar closest to the Aqua Théâtre stage, taking shots and watching the wonderful water-mixed-acrobatic dancing show right before us.

Our enjoyable time almost came to a screeching halt when Karen and Daniel suddenly appeared out of nowhere. They did not have a clue what was going on exactly or what we were doing. I suppose it would have looked strange to them seeing me all dolled up in my wedding dress—the exact dress I was supposed to walk down the aisle to their son in.

Emma quickly caught them up to what we were doing as Karen gave me a huge hug. She started bawling. It was getting close to dinnertime, and we told them we would see them shortly so that they would fuck off and leave us alone, try to get them to stop causing such a scene, which had become their usual behavior. I turned around and took another shot of alcohol. My buzz was immediately wearing off. I did in fact know how to manage my liquor. Suddenly, a wave of sadness came over me once I saw those two crying.

It was time to go for dinner. On our way back to our staterooms, however, we passed the karaoke bar, which was in full swing early this evening.

I looked at Emma, who knew exactly what I was already thinking.

"Should I?" I asked.

"You shall!" she replied.

So, all of us headed into the bar for a couple more songs—a few quick tunes. I could not let this dress go to waste without singing my heart out one last time.

I got on stage, and I could see and feel the wonder of the sparkles lighting it up and the room, playing off the spotlights and shining and sparkling against the bar walls.

I grabbed the microphone, the music played, and I started to sing the opening line to the song "My Heart Will Go On." Yes, I sang the song titled "My Heart Will Go On" by the talented Canadian, Celine Dion. I made it through entirely without crying and finished the song to roaring applause. I gave high fives and hugs off stage, and we said goodbye to our cruise ship friends and told them we would see them after dinner, likely.

We met everyone for the fancy casino night dinner, and it was spectacular because nobody was there besides my family and me. The Fishers, or Atticus's family, were busy at a live show that started at 6:00 p.m. They were too upset to come that night. That is why it was finally a great meal; I, and the rest of the crew, ate a ton of food—steak and lobster...scallops. It was a delicious seafood night.

Afterward, we all went for a walk with Callum along the top deck to look at the ocean and the stars. Also, my mom wanted a cigarette.

I remember asking her in so many ways and so many times during this trip, in these exact words...

"What would you do if you were me about Atticus?"

My parents were the only ones who never said one bad word about Atticus so far, the whole trip. They did not want to sway my decision.

They wanted me to produce my own decision, all on my own, about what to do. They knew annulment was floating high up in the air of my reality.

My mother took a long drag of her smoke and replied, "Well, like, he was not genuinely nice to you, was he? He is always making fun of you."

There it was, finally, something, some sort of truth from my mother. Something to open my eyes up to another opinion. She kept her opinions about our significant others always to herself. This was a piece of the puzzle I had not seen for myself because I was living it.

Of course, I had heard incessant, negative reasons from everybody else as to why I should not stay married to this man. I wanted my parents' opinion, and finally, I had something other than my typical Mom and Dad answer: "Do you love him?"

Of course I did, or else I would not be in this position and where I am today if I did not love him, but was love enough this time? And did I truly know what love meant at that moment of my life? I was incredibly young and naïve at that point in my life, and I already knew that. That was not the first time I had heard it, but it gave me a lot to ponder coming from my own mother.

My family wanted to first go play bingo (A huge hit on cruise ships. Do not knock it!). Then they were going to watch the Aqua Théâtre spectacular show. I let them continue without Callum and me. It was getting late, and I could see Callum was tired. He and I both. It was another eventful day. I took him back to our stateroom, gave him a bath, snuggled on my bed, read his favourite book, and watched a movie. Tonight's movie was Tarzan, the cartoon Disney version, of course. I held my sweet little sunshine in my arms and rocked him to sleep. I had too much on my mind to sleep that night. It was becoming clear to me that everybody witnessing Atticus and my relationship over the years had kept a lot of their opinions to themselves. Was I truly blinded by love? Was I putting up with what I didn't deserve all of these years? Was I perhaps doing just fine all on my own already?

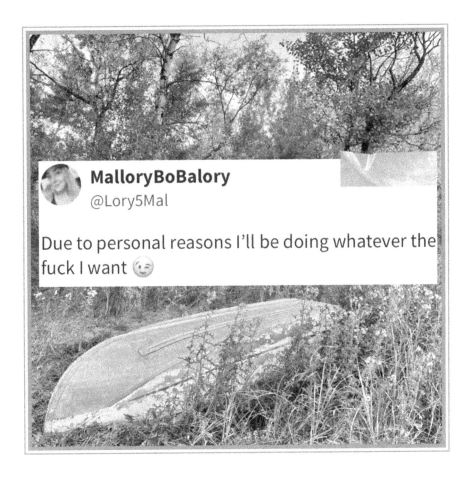

CHAPTER 14

Day 7 – Day Drunk at Sea

This day was the final day at sea. I was sitting on the balcony with Callum, and we were eating our breakfast and staring out at the ocean, searching for dolphins. In my head, I was searching for an answer as to what I was going to about my relationship with his father when we got home in a few days.

Atticus's family was calling my room that morning. They were already fighting over who would hang out with Callum for the day. I was told by my in-laws that I was "hogging" my own son. I didn't know there was such a thing or a phrase, honestly. How does a mother respond to that sort of statement?

Meanwhile, Callum was the only person keeping me sane on this massive boat but what felt like a cage at sea. He made me strong, for him and for myself. So, I compromised and let everybody know that I would be busy with Callum that morning, and we would meet them all at the buffet for lunch. From there, they could each take turns spending some time with him before the final supper.

With the day's plan in place, we headed to the waterslides and the pool, followed by ice cream and some mini golf together. Lunchtime came all too soon, and we were in the main restaurant at the front of the ship, eating a big lunch at the buffet, sitting next to the windows chatting and gazing out at sea for the last day. I could never get tired of that scenic ocean view.

Atticus's parents took Callum and his stroller with promises and bribes of fun times and ice cream.

"See you at supper," they replied.

My heart sank. What was I going to do with myself now? I was going to go sulk in my stateroom, I decided. I sat on my balcony, legs stretched out on the chair across from me. I pondered my life and what I was going to do with it once I got home. Would I choose annulment or marriage to this man who disappointed and broke my heart into a million pieces in more ways than one? Never in my life had I imagined divorce or an annulment. All I ever imagined was the picture-perfect wedding and marriage. I was weighing the pros and cons. Which column had more?

Through the foggy balcony divider, I spotted my mom's green menthol pack of cigarettes over on my parent's balcony next door. I reached my arm around to grab it. The craving for cigarettes hit me out of nowhere. I was smoking a drag when my parents entered the balcony.

"Let's get you out and do something!" they proclaimed after my mom finished a cigarette right along with me.

I was probing their brains yet again as to what I should do with Atticus when I got home. They offered the usual vague, nice, questionable answers again. No help.

That day, I was going to get day drunk, I decided. Maybe I'd get some sort of clarity, and why not? I had gone this far into the trip without getting too drunk or out of any sort of control. I wanted to enjoy a daytime pina colada and the Royal Meridian's tasty strawberry daiquiris—my sipping inspirations. We three made our way to the top of the deck bar, sipped our cocktails, and watched the wave riders. Dad and I tried out standing on the boards on the wave rider. I got knocked off immediately; we both did.

There was a zipline that went from one end of the ship to the other, gliding over the picturesque "solarium" at sea. Dad and I took a ride on the zipline. How could we go the whole trip without trying it out? My mom was too scared of heights and everything fun and adventurous to try it. Dad and I zipped across, flying high and free. It was a lot of fun for a moment.

Next, we escorted my mother to the "ship sale." The stores on the cruise ship were having a final day sale with fifty percent off. I wasn't in the mood for shopping, but a little retail therapy couldn't hurt. I found the cutest black-and-white polka dot purse in the Kate Spade store. I purchased it for myself immediately. What a great find. Dad and I continued on to drinking beers for the rest of the day. We were sitting in the levitating bar—yes, levitating. It rises ten floors and then brings you back down into the main foyer. This ship was magical, besides how they handled my wedding or lack thereof, of course.

"Dad, what should I do about Atticus?" I asked yet again. I'm sure he, along with everyone else, was so tired of talking about the matter. We all were consumed by it, though. It was constantly in the back of our minds, and at the forefront of mine.

"You know, I did a lot of stupid things when I was younger and got into a lot of fights. Atticus has a lot, and I mean a lot, of growing up to do—a ton. People make mistakes, though. Hopefully, they can learn and grow from them," he responded, taking a sip of his beer.

"Did you know that on the first night on the ship, Atticus had gotten back to our stateroom earlier than us and started blaring the music in your room while Callum was sleeping next door? I, and another crew member on the ship, had to go over and tell him to turn the music down," My dad explained.

A lot of growing up to do, indeed. He clearly was a very selfish man. This was repeated in so many ways, yet why couldn't they just tell me what to do? That's all I wanted. I understand they wanted me to come to a decision all on my own, and I was frustrated at the time but also respected that about my parents, and my family in general. We tended to stay far away from drama; let's live our most peaceful lives, please.

Mom was finished shopping, she found herself a nice brown-patterned Michael Kors purse, and now I had suddenly new information to ponder.

I was quite drunk at this point, walking back through the maze of the ginormous ship, down the long hallways to our staterooms. I needed to take a shower, get ready, and perhaps sober up before our final dinner with the crew…the Fisher crew. Fuck! They were the very last people I wanted to converse with on this ship! Final night, Mallory. You can do it. You can get through this. Get through the whispers at the other side of the table. The whispers they thought were unheard, that they thought I didn't notice. I was just simply there in body, something for them to watch and dissect from the other side of the table.

I was giving myself a pep talk. I had made it this far without losing it or becoming a blubbering mess publicly. I can do hard things, I told myself.

I grabbed a cocktail to drink and got ready in my room. The delicious cocktails just seemed to be endless that day! Oh, well. If there was any day to finally sip away, that was the day.

I had Callum's babysitters mapped out for the day and night. I was responsible for nobody but myself that night. I thought I needed more drinks to take the edge off. Really, I was very nervous going into dinner with Atticus's family. I mean, who wouldn't be? I didn't feel like having Karen's cell phone constantly shoved in my face again. I was emotionally fragile on that trip, and rightly so. I was about to go into the lion's den. Not quite literally, but that was the general feeling, and how my entire family described it even. I was preparing myself to be questioned about my future, my plans, my everything, to know everything and have it all figured out for everyone.

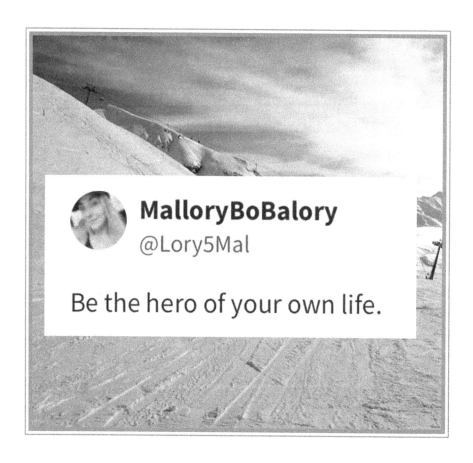

CHAPTER 15

Who's Going to Transport This Dress Now?

It was dinner time at our usual table, one last time, with the same amazing serving staff. They put on a spectacular final show.

All eyes were on me again that night. How was I managing things? What were my emotions like? I would like to think they were amazed at how well I was overseeing it all. I mean, they certainly would not have been able to manage this disaster of a situation better than I, that I can be certain of. Not this crowd. How entertaining I must have been for them to watch, speculate over, and stare at. I was something to do over dinner because their conversations were entirely dull. Besides the days that we got off the boat, typical conversations, of course, would be what each did with their day.

Enter in a snide comment from Karen: "Wish we could have—insert something— with our grandson." Complain some more, as if Callum could not understand their words or actions or feel their miserable vibe. They were the kind of people who were never completely happy or content in life.

On this last night, though, I could feel the stares all at once. I was just trying to eat my dinner and get through it. Everybody was staring (besides my family, of course), trying desperately to break the ice, and make things seem normal for Callum. None of this was normal. In fact, it was far from what some would call a normal vacation. A normal family destination wedding vacation was not in the cards for me. I decided to speak up for myself and give them something all to truly gawk at. Plus, I had a ton of liquid courage, aka I was on my second glass of delicious white wine for the night.

"Who is going to bring my dress back now?" I purposely blurted out at the table.

Everyone put their forks down, suddenly looking awkwardly at each other for the answer.

"Since Atticus was the one to carry it through for me, an extra pair of hands, now he is not here. I will need to push Callum in the stroller through the airport alone now. Who is up for the challenge?" I asked the table, clearly not meaning any of my family members, since the rest of them were all driving back home. It would be extremely easy for one of them to bring my dress home in their vehicle compared to me struggling with a wedding dress and a toddler through airport security, then carry-on. It definitely was not going to be stored in a bag at the bottom of the airplane to wreck and ruin.

Stunned silence. I love a good awkward moment. I know it might sound a little strange, but there is something internally funny to me about an openly awkward moment. Yes, I am a little weird; you are a little weird; we are all a little weird. Life's too short to be normal, I always say.

Carol piped up. "Bruce and I can take it in our truck."

"Perfect, right on. Thank you!" I exclaimed.

Our amazing waiter came by our table and placed my wedding cake right dab in the centre of the table. Unbeknownst to him, he said he almost forgot to bring it the other night. We all stared at the cake in awkward silence again. The only thing missing from the cake was the cake topper I had specially ordered. It was Cinderella and Prince Charming in their beautiful carriage.

"Welp, dig in, everybody!" I smiled and exclaimed.

Then I tossed my napkin over my empty plate on the table, got up, and left, telling nobody what I was doing or where I was going. I half sauntered, half stormed away. I was too nice of a person to actually storm away. That would be mean. I am not a mean person, quite the opposite. I was tired of being too damn nice, and exhausted from pretending the entire trip. I was overwhelmed with holding on and taking care, walking on eggshells over everybody else's emotions for seven long nights and six long days.

I snuck out of there, hoping everybody at the table would think I was going to the bathroom so nobody would follow me. I had had enough of these people, all people, this charade. I was drunk. I was over it, and I needed out of that fishbowl, away from the stares and the glares. Besides, I had finished my delicious steak already anyway. It was time for another drink, and I needed some fresh air. Better yet, I was craving a cigarette. So very badly. I needed to find one that instant.

Where did they sell cigarettes on a luxury cruise ship? I asked around at a few bars. No luck. No gift shops, and no tobacco anywhere. Where do people go to smoke, the top deck? Surely, I could find somebody smoking a cigarette up there. I had the most intense craving, and once again, I did not even smoke. I have never smoked as many dirty cigarettes as I did on that cruise ship and on that night. I needed some air badly and to see the dark sea at night one final time. I also really needed that cigarette.

Taylor Swift's music was playing loudly over the speakers on the top deck. The song where she's singing about standing in a nice dress and staring at the sunset, in your wildest dreams.

I sang along, standing at the ship's bow, looking over the edge at the vast sea of darkness, in my nice dress, staring at the sunset. Do I stay with Callum's dad or not? That was the ultimate question.

A dark older man with black hair was looking over the edge of the ship as well, puffing on a cigarette. Ah ha! I finally found a smoker.

He said his name was Danny, and he happily handed me over a cigarette. We contemplated life together that night. I sat and listened to him, his regrets, his dreams. He told me he was not a great man or a great father. His wife and kids left him, and he missed them terribly and regretted all his selfish decisions. He puffed at his cigarettes, offering me his life advice. He felt sorry for Atticus, naturally. Danny was a genuinely nice, kind man with the words of his life's wisdom. I pictured him as an older Atticus in this situation, puffing away, looking back at his own life regrets and thinking of all the ways he wished he could have treated me and his own son better. How he could have been around more. Been a more present father, and lover, not a selfish one. Make us a priority. He had a tremendous amount of growing up to do. I told Danny about my cruise ship debacle and the debates going on in my mind about what to do about the whole situation. He offered me his advice, which was to give Atticus another chance as he wished he would have gotten. I listened mostly because he was a nice man, but mostly because I enjoyed having a cigarette away from everyone on the top of the ship.

"Mallory!"

I heard my name, turned around, and my parents were there. They were looking for me. How long was I sitting here for?

"Bye, Danny. It was nice meeting you. I hope you enjoy the rest of your vacation. Thanks for the cigarettes and chat," I spoke.

He smiled and waved goodbye. "Don't forget now what I told you!" he said with seemingly immense importance. "I won't," I yelled back, turning to walk with my parents. I already had forgotten, though; I did not know what he, in fact, wanted me to remember. I chuckled to myself; this was all very random.

My mom was beyond worried. I do not know what she thought I would do on my own. I was a grown-ass woman, for fuck's sake. She did not need to be this worried about me wandering away from that stuffy table to get some fresh fucking air or cigarettes, I suppose. I told her this so that she would calm her nerves down. She was anxiously smoking her cigarette. I thought I might as well join her one last time.

We walked back to our rooms together. Callum was already asleep in their room with Emma and Ledger. I had my own room all to myself for the night. Sitting on the bed in my dress, drunk and alone, I decided that was the night to call Atticus. Why the fuck not? I had so much on my mind and so many things to say to him.

I grabbed the phone beside the bed. How did one call internationally? From a ship? Could you call people from the middle of the ocean? You must remember this was not a time when cellphones held the communicative power that they do nowadays. I had my cellphone shut off, so I did not get charged roaming fees from being in the middle of the sea, searching for cellular service. Plus, I knew that I would be heartbroken by the massive number of congratulatory texts I would receive from friends and family back home, asking how the wedding went… Or why it did not happen at all.

I dialed his number correctly, and it was ringing. I was pleased with myself. I was not as drunk as I suspected after all, perhaps. Then I heard his voice.

I instantly started crying. "How could you do this to me?"

"I love you so much. I'm going to spend the rest of my life making this up to you, I promise," he proclaimed.

He went on about how he loved me so much. He also dove into his struggles getting home and how sad and lonely he was. I did not want to hear of his misery because what about mine? This was my dream he crushed here! I told him he needed to get out of our house, out of our home once Callum and I got back into the country. I figured I was too drunk to continue this conversation. Instantly, I was so upset I could barely speak. Hearing his voice crushed me all over again inside, thinking of what could have been, what should have been.

I said goodbye and hung up the phone. I did not know how much money I was being charged for this late, obnoxious, drunk phone call of mine, and I did not need to rack up the bill any more than I already had this trip.

I was bawling by myself for what felt like hours. I must have eventually passed out asleep. I woke up the next morning still wearing my beautiful dress, so I must have finally gotten some sleep, at least I thought. There was one good thing.

CHAPTER 16

The Day Harry Potter Saved My Life

Day 8   <u>Fort Lauderdale, Florida</u>   6:15AM

*W*e docked early morning 5:00 a.m. I was like Cinderella singing to the birds that morning. I wasn't hungover. Extremely tired, yes, but I was finally getting off this boat.

I have never been more excited to get off a luxury cruise ship in my life than at that moment. I could not sleep that last night, or any night really, since we set foot on the ship. No more of my husband's family to deal with, no more sulking around the beautiful ship full of reminders of what should have been, what could have been. No more trying to cover my tears and baggy eyes in front of a massive number of happy travellers. No more pretending.

Most important of all, though, I was, for the first time, feeling something other than sadness and sorrow. I was excited to go to Harry Potter World. Yes, that was what got me through not throwing myself overboard, Harry Potter. Universal Studios and Islands of Adventure here we freaking come! We were going to drop our luggage off and get into our cozy theme park clothes and ride all the rides. I had already purchased our passes for two days and two parks, which happened to be right next to each other. We were staying at the Royal Lowes Pacific Resort which is a stone's throw away from the theme park. They have a walking path connected right to the parks. You also get to use your room key to butt to the front of the lines, and yes, it is just magically incredible. Universal Studios had just recently added an entirely new section of the park dedicated to Harry Potter World. It was Diagon Alley, and they had the dragon on top of Gringotts Bank, blowing real fire. You got to ride the Hogwart's Express to and from the parks, and I will just stop there because I could draft an entire novel of my Potterhead fandom. What I am trying to get at here, though, is that Harry Potter truly saved my life that day, that trip, that nightmare of a vacation. It was the first time I legitimately smiled all trip when Callum, my parents, and I were getting a picture right next to the "Night Bus." The magical life-like talking head started talking to me.

When I had my back turned to his tiny scrunched-up face, he yelled, "Hey, you there, you have the dark mark. She has the dark mark!" He was referring to my gigantic rose tattoo on my upper left back. An incredibly amazing nerdy reference of having the dark mark, meaning I am also a wizard!

I turned to him and grinned. "Yes, keep talking to me! This is my dream come true!" Harry Potter life-like character talking to me.

He asked where I was from. Canada. I will never forget that moment. I have the photograph framed up on the wall in my home to remind myself…keep going, I can do hard things, and there will be better, happier times through the storm. I would get married at Hogwarts Castle if I could someday. Hey, now I can.

One bummer, of course, was the fact that I had spent over $1000.00 on Atticus's park passes, and they would not give me a refund. So that is another expense I had to eat there. Besides that, it was worth it. I am so glad that I got to experience the magic with my son.

We spent two wonderful days back and forth between the two parks, riding all the rides over and over. I bought so much Harry Potter merchandise. The retail therapy in that store was out of control but necessary.

CHAPTER 17

Homeward Bound

Flying home with my son in my arms made me rein back the tears that I wanted to shed for my new, questionable, unknown life. I had kicked his immature father out of our house; our relationship was up in the air, in limbo. What was I going to do? I needed to take my time and make the right decision. Should I get an annulment? Time allotted would make it easy to just pretend this whole nightmare did not even happen. Was this the ultimate red flag?

I walked into the house to a ton of roses, and there were rose petals all over the floor leading to my bedroom and to a new nightstand. Wow. Sorry I ruined the best day of your life and fucked up our entire vacation, so here is a new fucking nightstand? What the actual fuck? Whatever. I was exhausted. I turned on my phone for the first time with hundreds of messages, mostly from Atticus, of course.

Atticus was living at his brother's house for the time being. So, over the next few days, Atticus came over, begged and pleaded, and pleaded, and begged. My friends came over for wine nights to let me vent my entire story. I just wanted them to tell me what to do. I wanted somebody to tell me what to do.

One evening my best friends Annalise, Jessica, and Aurora, who I mentioned at the start of this novel, came over with bottles of wine to watch my "not so wedding slideshow." We laughed, we cried, and we all could not believe what had just happened. It was surreal, like I was living a different life just straight out of a movie.

Atticus and his friends seemed to think that I owed them a thank you for, I suppose, "looking after him" and also "picking him up from the airport." Fuck off. I could not give a flying fuck if he had to hitchhike home. That was the last thing on my mind. I needed to put myself first, my son first, and what our future would look like first, not caring what other people thought or people who barely knew me, swaying any decision of mine.

I went to therapy for the first time in my life. I spoke to therapists, and I so desperately wanted them to tell me what to do. The underlying response that kept coming up was that I deserved better. I was weighing my decision of leaving or staying for the sake of our son. This boy, Atticus, had a lot of growing up to do to become a man still. I knew it deep down in my heart. But what about our family? We had already started growing together. I so desperately wanted Callum to have a little sibling. How long would that take, and what about Callum?

Allow me to quote a scene from the movie *Titanic* when an older Rose says, "A woman's heart is a deep ocean of secrets."

Well, now I've let you all, dear readers, in on mine. My deepest secret. I lead with my head instead of my heart.

I let Atticus move back in two months after the cruise ship disaster. We didn't have the physical wedding. Legally, we were married according to the paperwork we completed prior to our journey to Florida. We had another beautiful boy less than a year later, and that is why this was all meant to be. I've always wanted to have two children and felt like it was my destiny to be a mother of two wonderful little boys.

If I had not met or married Atticus, I would not have the two best little human beings in my life forever—Callum and Walker. I live and breathe for my kids. They give me life, and they fulfilled my dreams of becoming the mother I have always wanted to be.

My whole entire world is my boys, and for them, it was all worth it in the end.

We have raised Callum to become his own person. He has the biggest heart. He's the kind of kid who stands up for his friends and other people on the playground or anywhere in life. He's a great human being, and I'm so proud to be Callum's mother! It's my greatest accomplishment in life truly, becoming Callum and Walker's mom, just watching them grow into these great human beings!

CHAPTER 18

More Mallory

I hope you enjoyed my wildly true story, dear reader. I have more writing and stories of mine in the works, so stay tuned! Follow me on Instagram @mallorybobalory. Visit <u>www.mallorybobalory.org</u> to read my blogs and take a look at my outdoor photography captures and entertainment! Visit my online store featuring organic and eco-friendly products at Mallory's Adventures Store.

https://mallory-s-adventures.myshopify.com

Let's all try to live sustainably and shop for organic, recycled products whenever we can. Little daily efforts help make our world a much better place. Be kind to everyone always. Most important of all, be *you*!

CPSIA information can be obtained
at www.ICGtesting.com
Printed in the USA
LVHW100900090722
722950LV00034B/47